Love is the Answer to Your Prayers

Spiritual Meditation Book, Relationship With God

Charlene M. Mathews

© **Copyright 2022 - All rights reserved.**

The content contained within this book may not be reproduced, duplicated or transmitted without direct written permission from the author or the publisher.

Under no circumstances will any blame or legal responsibility be held against the publisher, or author, for any damages, reparation, or monetary loss due to the information contained within this book, either directly or indirectly.

Legal Notice:

This book is copyright protected. It is only for personal use. You cannot amend, distribute, sell, use, quote or paraphrase any part, or the content within this book, without the consent of the author or publisher.

Disclaimer Notice:

Please note the information contained within this document is for educational and entertainment purposes only. All effort has been executed to present accurate, up to date, reliable, complete information. No warranties of any kind are declared or implied. Readers acknowledge that the author is not engaged in the rendering of legal, financial, medical or professional advice. The content within this book has been derived from various sources. Please consult a licensed professional before attempting any techniques outlined in this book.

By reading this document, the reader agrees that under no circumstances is the author responsible for any losses, direct or indirect, that are incurred as a result of the use of the information contained within this document, including, but not limited to, errors, omissions, or inaccuracies.

Table of Contents

INTRODUCTION 1

PROLOGUE 5

CHAPTER 1: KNOWING ONESELF 13
    CULTIVATING SELF-LOVE 14
    UPROOTING CHILDHOOD TRAUMAS 18
    KNOWING YOUR TRIGGERS 20
    FALLING IN LOVE WITH YOUR FLAWS 21
    PRACTICAL EXERCISE 23

CHAPTER 2: MOLDING YOUR RELATIONSHIP WITH GOD 25
    COMMUNING WITH GOD 26
    DEMYSTIFYING THE MYTH OF GOD 28
    DISCOVERING GOD'S PLAN FOR YOUR LIFE 29
    PRACTICAL EXERCISE 31

CHAPTER 3: BECOMING ONE WITH THE UNIVERSE 33
    CONSCIOUSNESS 35
    PRACTICING MINDFULNESS 36
    LIVING IN THE MOMENT 41
    PRACTICAL EXERCISE 42

CHAPTER 4: SOLO SPIRITUAL JOURNEY 43
    RELIGIOUS DENOMINATIONS 45
        Discovering Your Spiritual Preference 47
    COMMUNAL SPIRITUALITY VS. INDIVIDUAL SPIRITUALITY 48
    PRACTICAL EXERCISE 50

CHAPTER 5: YOUR EGO MAY DESTROY YOU 51
    MYTHS ABOUT EGO 52
    BEING EGO DRIVEN VS. PURPOSE DRIVEN 53
    HOW TO CONTROL YOUR EGO 54
    BALANCING SELF-LOVE WITH SELFLESSNESS 56
    PRACTICAL EXERCISE 57

CHAPTER 6: SIMPLE ACTS OF LOVE 59

My Brother's Keeper	60
Different Love Languages	63
Unlearning Toxic Love	65
Practical Exercise	66

CHAPTER 7: FINDING PURPOSE THROUGH LOVE 67

Know Your Tribe	69
Purposeful Careers	70
Community-Based Social Impact Programs	*71*
Using Your Gifts and Talents to Benefit Others	72
Practical Exercise	73

CONCLUSION 75

REFERENCES 79

Introduction

The world's greatest musicians have sung about the power of love, poets have intricately put together words to describe that feeling of being in love, love has become something that we easily associate with a romantic feeling towards a loved one. It is the reality of our lives; we have normalized the concept of falling in love with a significant other and have completely forgotten that there are so many other forms of love.

Love should not be limited to the theory we read in books, the beautiful Instagram pictures of married couples we see as we scroll through social media, or the grand wedding celebrations that are supposed to be a public declaration of love. Our measure of love has somehow been belittled to the materialistic things that the world has to offer us, we have somehow forgotten that God showed us the biggest expression of love when He sent His only son to die for our sins. For some of the readers that are not spiritual, it may be hard to imagine that something so divine as sacrificing your only son can be translated as a measure of love. We hope by the end of this book, you realize how God's sacrifice of His son, His relationship with humankind, is the greatest love story to ever be written.

The purpose of this book is to re-define the meaning of love in accordance with what God desires from us. The simplest acts of love you may do today is pick up after yourself when you eat from a public space, or give your last penny to the stranger that sits across the road while you drive to work. It may not be as divine as sacrificing your own son, but it's close to the likeness of God. By picking up after yourself, you show appreciation for the work done by the cleaners, and that last penny you give to that homeless person might be the reason they start to believe that better days are coming.

The measure of love should be how we show up for other people when there is no one watching or giving us praise. Many people believe they can only show love to strangers with the expectation of applause from society, but this love is conditional and it is self-seeking. The Bible has the best definition of love in 1 Corinthians 13:4-8 which reads (ESV):

> *"Love is patient, love is kind. It does not envy, it does not boast, it is not proud. It does not dishonor others, it is not self-seeking, it is not easily angered, it keeps no record of wrongs. Love does not delight in evil but rejoices with the truth. It always protects, always trusts, always hopes, always perseveres."*

The kind of love described in the Bible is what God expects from us when we deal with our loved ones, when we deal with strangers on the way to work, the people who are undeserving of love, to mention but a few. God does not promise to only love us when we are good, He loves us regardless. His love is unconditional. Our human nature is often inherently selfish. We are easily distracted by our selfish egos and we struggle to love other people the way God loves us.

This book will teach all readers how to be more compassionate when dealing with people. In the course of a stressful day, it is easy to react irrationally and feel entitled to our own feelings. The bigger picture is always about how we are able to develop an attitude of emotional intelligence in situations where our humanity would cause us to have emotional reactions in stressful situations. Think about the last time you felt like you reacted in a rude manner, how long did it take to react? If you notice, our emotions can easily dictate our actions, it takes a mere second to lush out of anger and it takes years to cultivate patience.

Love is the strongest emotion–it can either build you or break you. The purpose of this book is to expand the idea of love from the box that society has placed it in. Love should not be limited to the romantic attachment to somebody else. It should be a core principle of life. From the moment each of us wake up, we should tackle the new day with love, brush our teeth with love, drive to work or school with love, associate with other people with love, then return home with lessons to be better for the following day. The great news is that each and every one of us has the capacity to love, we have to know that love is limitless.

In order for this love to overflow to others, we need to love ourselves first through accepting our character shortcomings and forgiving ourselves for our past mistakes. Cultivating self-love means delving into our past, discovering what childhood traumas we might still need to heal from, and working on uprooting those toxic traits. If you were raised in an environment where you had to earn love, you probably still struggle to love other people unconditionally. The Bible teaches us how to love other people without any expectation of a reward. To be able to learn this type of love, we need to embark on a spiritual journey with God where we let go of our selfish desires and focus on how we can please God by loving others unconditionally. In Corinthians 13:13, the Bible continues to emphasize that: "And now these three remain: faith, hope and love. But the greatest of these is love" (ESV).

Prologue

Jane woke up that Sunday morning feeling a little thrown off balance, her alarm had gone off at around 6 a.m., which is the time she usually woke up for work, except that today was not a working day. She worked as a Registered Nurse at the local Elmsdale Hospital. She had been working there for over 10 years, since her graduation from Elmsdale School of Nursing. Jane's husband, Peter, was working out of town again. He was a site engineer who was often sent to work out of town because of his expertise. Jane met Peter while she was in her final year of nursing school, up until then, she had no intention of getting to know anyone on a long-term basis. She had dated a few of her classmates during the early years of her school, but she soon gave it up as they all ended up taking advantage of her.

Peter bumped into her at the local hospital while she was completing her training. He came in through the emergency room with a broken leg that he had sustained while working on a construction site. Their first encounter was a blur for Peter since he was high on morphine. She, on the other hand, was working a late-night shift when she was assigned a 29-year-old male, broken leg, vitals stable who just needed observation for the next few weeks. When Jane walked into Peter's room, she noticed that he had sustained an open fracture to his leg which had now been suspended in the air to reduce pressure on it, and Peter was passed out. She immediately noticed a slight discoloration around the area where the doctors had positioned the splint. Her first instinct was to request antibiotics from the doctor, but upon a closer look, she realized the wound was not infected. As she was busy monitoring his vitals, Peter sluggishly whispered, "Can I please have some water, young lady?" The rest seems like history to her now.

Three years after their initial encounter, they got married at the local church right next to her nursing school. Peter was extremely religious and, therefore, suggested that they get married within a year of their encounter. Jane was only 25-years-old at that time and was overwhelmed with emotion that a gentleman was interested in a plain Jane like her. She grew up in a broken family and somewhere along the way, she believed she would never get married to a man that did not value her as a woman. Her father had been both physically and emotionally abusive to her mother. She had such a messed-up idea of what love was. One thing she noticed from her previous relationships was the fact that she did not want to commit to any of them despite their constant demands for commitment. She viewed marriage as a prison where a woman was not allowed to explore her career options beyond the job of being a mother.

On the day of their wedding, she made a vow to herself–to always love herself more than her husband would ever be able to love her. She knew that Peter was a different man from the man her father was, that was one of the reasons she married him. For starters, he was very intrigued by the fact that she was a registered nurse, and he was very receptive to her feelings. She was around the age of 28 when she got pregnant with their first child, Nelly, who was born in the summer of 2005 at the same hospital Jane's mother had given birth too. She was hit with a wave of emotion the day the doctor placed her daughter in her arms, she suddenly realized that she had never loved anyone as much as she was going to love her daughter. Her husband, Peter, was so excited that he held Nelly for over 30 minutes, swaying her beautiful face front and back. The sun rays shone their way through the hospital window and fell beautifully on her daughter's head, highlighting her full head of curly hair that she got from her father. Jane had never seen anything as beautiful as her daughter, if she ever doubted her beauty, her daughter was proof that there could be beauty born out of ashes.

During the first two years of their daughter's life, Jane and Peter could barely take their eyes off of Nelly. Jane would usually be up by 6 a.m. to prepare Nelly's bag for daycare every day. Peter would help her prepare the baby's lunch the day before, and by 7 a.m. they would all be on the road to their respective places. Jane would take Nelly with her to the daycare provided by her workplace, while Peter would anticipate seeing both his girls again at the end of the day. Watching Peter be a fully involved father with his daughter at such a young age made Jane's heart ache for the love she never got as a child from her father, she envied Nelly and was also extremely happy that she got to understand what love meant from a young age. She wishes her mother was there to watch her granddaughter break the chains of absent fathers in their generation, but her mom had passed away just before she had enrolled in nursing school.

Jane had to re-learn how to love all over again, this time around she learned from her daughter's little heart. Nelly was such a kind baby; she was very aware of her surroundings. She loved playing with the morning sun rays as they hit her crib, she would lay in bed self-soothing until her mom came to pick her up. Where Jane lacked in patience, Nelly's calm demeanor reminded her that she could maybe work on her patience when she was dealing with those hardheaded patients that kept her running during her shifts. Besides the rare long nights, Jane loved her life as a mother of one, and she loved her husband even more as a father to her daughter. It was through watching his love for Nelly that Jane was forced to deal with certain aspects of her childhood trauma. She realized that her overcompensation and constant need to seek validation was because she always had to try to earn her father's love as a child.

In the summer of 2008, Nelly had turned three years old, that is when Jane realized that she was pregnant with their second child. She was completely caught off guard since she was sure that she had taken her birth control. It was also the end of Peter's paternity leave; he was being stationed back to the sites out of town which meant that she had to learn how to juggle her responsibilities as a mother and as a full-time nurse. That evening, when Peter returned home, she gave him the news about the second child. Peter was immediately overjoyed to know that they were going to be parents again. Then, it suddenly hit him that he would be away for most of the pregnancy, and this did not sit well with him. As he had been there for every single milestone for his daughter and he wanted to do that for his second child as well. That night they both got down on their knees to ask God for guidance on what to do. Jane wanted Peter to ask to be relocated back to the jobs close to Elmsdale, while Peter was torn between the good pay that came from site jobs and being emotionally and physically available for his wife during her second pregnancy. With the new baby coming, they both knew they needed more income in order to make ends meet, Nelly was starting preschool soon and that in itself was another expense they had temporarily forgotten.

After a week of prayer, they both agreed that Peter would continue his current job but with the condition that he was home twice a month to check on both his girls and the baby that was baking. They were relieved to know that at least things were looking up. Nelly was at that inquisitive age of three, and on the night before her dad left, she asked him to read her favorite bedtime story. Although her mind could not comprehend what two weeks away from home would mean, she knew that her dad's presence would be missed. She loved having both mommy and daddy tuck her into bed and tonight, only daddy tucked her in. Nelly could also tell that her mommy was a bit nervous about dad being away, but she had told her mommy that she would give her big hugs whenever she missed daddy.

Jane's first trimester started off at a high note, unlike the first pregnancy, she felt nauseated all the time, she could not stand the smell of freshly baked pancakes that Nelly always asked for in the morning and she hated the commute to work. Nelly had started preschool, and yet again. Her hospital offered those services just opposite the hospital. She would often check-in on Nelly during her breaks and they would have lunch together, except this week she could only get the apple down because she kept throwing up. She did not want to worry Nelly, so she would tell her that she was not really hungry, therefore, she just needed a bite of an apple. The first two weeks with Peter being away felt like time had slowed down. She kept getting flashbacks of watching her mother struggle through the early stages of her pregnancy with Jane's sister. She was only five-years-old at that time, and her mom only told her that she had a bad tummy ache saying, "There is nothing to worry about, sweetie."

Peter came home as soon as he heard that Jane had been admitted to hospital for an emergency surgery. Jane had been diagnosed with an ectopic pregnancy. According to the doctors, the IUD that she had been using had shifted its position and that is why she had become pregnant while on birth control. The doctors had tried to administer a methotrexate injection but the pregnancy was not successfully eliminated. They discovered that her fallopian tubes had burst and an emergency surgery had to be done to save her life. Peter rushed straight into the hospital hallway requesting for his wife, his adrenaline had spiked and he was sweating profusely. He had only left his home for two weeks and returned to find his wife in surgery fighting for her life.

Nelly was still at her preschool for the day, he was asked by the staff to collect her while his wife was still in surgery. He could not dare to walk away from the hospital where his wife lay fighting for her life, but as he walked to the preschool to collect his daughter, he immediately regretted accepting the site job because he felt like it had cost him his unborn child. All he needed to hear was that Jane had survived the surgery, regardless of whether they would be able to have children or not in the future. Peter rushed back in with his daughter Nelly in his arms as he approached the doctor on-call who was ready to give him updates about the results from the surgery at that point.

"Are you Mr. Peter Brown?" the doctor asked sheepishly. Before Peter could respond, he asked him one single question, "Is she alive or not?" and the shy doctor nodded yes which further confused Peter because he didn't know whether the yes was that she was dead or yes, she was alive. Peter lost his patience and immediately asked to see his wife who was now lying in the recovery room. As he was busy looking at his wife's pale face, he grew more impatient. He needed the doctor to deliver the news before he could collect his daughter from the play pen where he had left her to save her from any emotional trauma at the hospital. It turns out the man who had asked him if he was Mr. Brown was merely an intern who was waiting for the superintendent on duty to brief Peter about Jane's surgery.

As Peter stood by his wife's side, he watched the monitors beep and prayed to God to keep her vitals stable. He was angry at God for giving them the go ahead about taking the site job and then letting Him desert his wife during the most vulnerable time of her pregnancy. Finally, after ten minutes of waiting the superintendent came in and told him that Jane had ruptured one of her fallopian tubes. She suffered a lot of bleeding but they were able to operate successfully and that she would be able to recover in a few days to be cleared to go home. Peter gave his first sigh of relief as he looked at his wife lying helplessly on that hospital bed. He remembered the last time they had been there; he was rocking his baby back and forth in the bright sun rays that fell into the room. He was searching for those same sun rays to fall on his wife's face because she looked so pale.

Days turned into weeks as Jane's body slowly recovered from the emergency surgery. Peter spent most of his days at the hospital lying right next to his wife. She would come out of her sleep unaware of her surroundings but seeing that her husband was standing right next to her bed. She would often nudge at his finger when he spoke to her, just to acknowledge that she could hear and understand what he was saying, her body just could not let her verbally respond. While she lay there recovering, Jane was dealing with a tremendous amount of emotions that she had no ability to express, due to her medical condition she could barely make any movements. She was screaming on the inside grieving the loss of her unborn child, and at the same time questioning her belief in God.

She felt somehow resentful towards her husband for not being around when she needed him the most. She also felt guilty for placing that burden on him because they had reached the decision together that he should return to the site. Jane had a small history of religion in her life, she had attended Catholic school as a toddler and had learned all about the rosary and the workings of the catholic church. She remembers hating the duration of the mass because the priest barely interpreted any of the scriptures for them. They were expected to attend catechist classes in preparation for the next sacrament which was the first communion. Religion was something her father had forced on her and he would use it as bait to get her attention, however much she had tried to impress him, he barely recognized her effort. In that moment while she lay in the hospital bed, Jane recited her Hail Mary's and begged the "Catholic God," as she had referred to him as a child, to help her get through this phase of her life.

She was drowning in utter despair, questioning her religion and trying to understand why God would let bad things happen to such a young couple like them. They prayed every day, they tithed every month, and made sure they helped out at church whenever they were needed. How was she going to cope with another loss after only having recently recovered from her mother's death–who she had mourned for several years. She needed to be an available mother to her surviving daughter, Nelly, a good wife to her grieving husband Peter and also a good work colleague to her co-workers at the hospital. Her husband re-introduced the idea of religion while they were dating, he was very open minded about the existence of one God for all of us. He prayed to God, and also believed in the divine nature of the universe. Peter always seemed to be more grounded than any other men she had met. She was now certain it was because he was sure of his religion, he knew how to pray and how to wait in hard times.

As soon as Jane hit the three-month mark post-surgery, she was cleared to resume her normal routine as a nurse starting with light-duty. Peter had decided to permanently move back home in order to offer spiritual and emotional support to his grieving wife. Their once easy lives had a major turn of events when they realized that they had lost their second baby, half their money had been used on Jane for her surgery, and they were not even sure they would be able to conceive naturally again. The first thing she dealt with, when she could, was to start engaging in mindful exercise with her small family. They woke up every Saturday to take a nature walk, to seek God, and to allow themselves to become one with the universe.

She also decided she needed to reach out to her father to resolve the childhood trauma that resided inside of her. She needed to ask him why he treated her mom so badly and to pour some of her new found love into him, she believed that people like him needed to be loved the most. She wondered if her father would ever ask for her forgiveness, but regardless, that was not part of her needs. She needed to face her childhood trauma and stop running away from it. She wanted her daughter to learn about the importance of forgiveness and to develop a relationship with her grandfather while they still had time on earth. As the days went by, Jane learned not to take any day for granted, she whispered words of affirmation to herself every morning, she reminded herself that she was not the reason they lost their baby and she believed that God would bless them in due time.

In November 2011, almost two years had passed since the terrible loss of their unborn child, Jane had taken a spiritual journey for over six months in search of answers about God, human existence, the reason why we go through loss, grief counseling, and learning to hope for the future. Peter had taken on the role of a full-time parent while Jane was embarking on her spiritual journey. They kept in contact every day as Nelly turned six. She was now in kindergarten and was the brightest child in her class. She had not been told about her mother's pregnancy, therefore, all she knew at that age was that mommy had to go build a relationship with God while healing from her surgery. Peter prepared a home-cooked meal for Jane at the end of her spiritual journey. She came home during February of 2012; it was their first Valentine's Day celebration post the loss of their child. They had both found ways of healing and were completely in love with themselves for making it through the rough patch. Nine months after her return, Jane gave birth to a bouncing baby boy who they named Aaron meaning a miracle from God.

Chapter 1:

Knowing Oneself

Give yourself the same care and attention that you give to others and watch yourself bloom. –Unknown

While some people believe that in order to find oneself, one has to fall in love with their perfect partner, this way their partner may help them become a better version of themselves, the reverse is true. For one to be able to love others, they need to love themselves first, no one can pour from an empty cup. The Bible itself says, "Out of the abundance of the heart, the mouth speaks," which means a heart full of hate will only spill hatred to others, a heart full of love will pour love unto others (Matthew 12:34 ESV). This is why it is important for everyone to learn to love themselves and embark on a journey of discovering self-love.

Think about what self-love means to you. For some people, it may take the form of self-care at a spa, and for others it may take the mental form of setting the appropriate boundaries. We all have different ways of showing ourselves love, but how many people know what it means to truly love yourself for your flaws? Knowing oneself is a much deeper journey of self-searching, much deeper than discovering your favorite movie or your least favorite meal. It's about knowing what makes you truly happy, what triggers you the most, what your biggest fears are, your strengths and weaknesses, to mention only a few.

The beauty of life is that it keeps unfolding, our character traits are always evolving with every challenge that life throws at us. The tough days may make some develop thicker skin while others become meek with the fear of the unknown. These layers of skin build as one continues to navigate the challenges of life, they may even give one a false sense of security, and yet crumble at any given moment of inconvenience. This is when you find yourself screaming at your cleaning lady when she misses a spot or blowing a small work inconvenience out of proportion. Knowing yourself gives you the power to master your emotions, to take charge of emotions that would have thrown you off balance, and in essence, teach you to pour that self-confidence into other people.

The journey of self-love will be the beginning of creating your own reality and listening to the universe to direct your purpose. When we walk on purpose, we walk in accordance with God's will for our lives. Finding your own purpose will bring fulfillment in your own life, it is from knowing oneself that one discovers their true purpose. Some people have to go through several closed doors before they realize that the external worldly things can never help them realize their purpose. It is from searching within oneself, facing one's own demons, and uprooting unresolved childhood trauma that one can shed off the walls that keep them from loving other people. In this chapter, we will elaborate on how God's love can help us discover our true selves, to see ourselves through our past trauma, and embark on the journey of healing.

Cultivating Self-Love

According to the Oxford dictionary, self-love is described as the focus on one's own happiness to the exclusion of others (2022). This means that a person has to cultivate the spirit of putting their needs first every once in a while, even if they have been conditioned to prioritize other people's feelings to the expense of their own. The irony of our human nature is we are always so quick to care for the needs of others. We have somehow been conditioned to think that we receive some sort of redemption from making sacrifices for others without consideration for personal needs.

Our lives are made up of the relationships we form with other people, whether it is family members, friendships, or acquaintances, we are all interrelated in a way. We usually value these relationships and forget that the most important relationship a person can have is the relationship with oneself. The relationship between your mind, body, and soul is for a lifetime, none of us can live authentically without having those three aspects of the self-aligned. Take the example of the relationship between husband and wife, it is ordained by God to remain permanent, both partners vow to stick together in sickness and in health until they die. That is a lifetime commitment which is easily made to somebody else, the underlying motive being love. Have you ever stopped to wonder why we rarely make that kind of commitment to ourselves?

When we speak of building a relationship with the self, the three aspects we spoke about in the previous paragraph come into play. The first aspect is learning to communicate with self-compassion to your own mind, basically practicing mindfulness through teaching our minds to think positively about ourselves. According to the University of Minnesota's Center for Spirituality and Healing, distinction was made between the mind and the brain stating that while the mind is the center of our emotional consciousness, the brain allows us to experience different forms of emotion (Hart, 2019). Our thoughts have a major impact on the way we get through our days, it is normal to feel overwhelmed when life is not going as planned. Negative thoughts can arise leading to feelings of low self-esteem. These feelings may become so repetitive that a person does not realize when they are projecting their negativity towards other people.

The second relationship to nurture is the one we have with our souls, which we usually refer to as our spirituality. A soul is defined as that part of our human bodies that is connected to our emotions and intellect, it is the source of a person's identity and comprises that small inner voice of reason when in situations that require thought and action (Merriam-Webster, 2019). In the Bible, this spiritual relationship is guided by the Holy Spirit, when God sent His son to die for our sins, we received the gift of the Holy Spirit on the Day of Pentecost. Our lives have unfortunately been so consumed with worldly matters that most people rarely listen to this Divine Voice, they cannot differentiate it from the voice of their ego.

In the later chapters to come, we will delve into how one can nurture their spirit by embarking on a spiritual journey, but for now, it is important to know that the mind and spirit perform different roles as they all work together to ensure that a person lives an authentic and purpose-driven life. Without a spiritual connection, we become slaves to our emotions which weakens our relationships with other people in the long run. Your attitude can affect the people around you for better or for worse. We need to change the narrative that somehow our emotions are inferior to intellect, mindful exercises would require that one acknowledges each emotion as they experience it, even if our emotions are ever-changing, the way we handle them will help us handle stressful situations better when relating to other people.

The third and final relationship with the self is the one we have with our physical bodies. The body is the outer physical embodiment of ourselves, it is the vessel that holds our entire existence together, the mind and soul cannot exist without a healthy body. The relationship a person shares with their body is one of the most important aspects in their journey to developing self-love, very often people that are physically insecure about their body weight, height, skin complexion, etc. will be more prone to developing feelings of self-hate. These feelings develop into deep hatred that spills into every aspect of that person's life. The good news is out of the three aspects of self, the body is usually the easiest aspect to be taken care of in case of a physical problem. The physical activities that we engage in have the ability to create a positive impact on our emotional and mental wellbeing, in other words, the mind is receptive to whatever energy the body provides.

Fortunately, our minds are like sponges, they can be molded into a more positive approach when these feelings of negativity arise. Some of the few activities that can help you break the loop of negative thoughts may include:

1. Practicing affirmations

    An affirmation is a daily pep talk that you give yourself at certain times during the day. It can be very early in the morning

before you get up to shower, recite your favorite Bible verse depending on what you feel you need assurance on for that day. The Bible has several categories of verses, from hope, happiness, healing, and strength. God made such writings so that we have spiritual guidance in our times of need. An affirmation can be as easy as "I am worthy of love;" "I am destined for great things;" "I am more than capable of accomplishing anything I set my mind to".

2. Practicing patience

As you begin these daily practices, do not expect to become an expert after a few days of trying. Our brains are wired over a period of time, it may take a while to rewire how your brain thinks, therefore, give yourself a grace period for the adjustment. Every goal in life requires conscious preparation, you've probably heard of the saying, "Rome was not built in a day," picture this journey as a building project where you lay one brick at a time. You cannot skip all the way from the foundation to the top. In a world that moves really fast, it is important to learn how to slow down, take a few deep breaths, and live in that particular moment. In the moment before you attain your goal weight, the moment when you're most depressed, take a moment to breathe and let life play itself out.

3. Teach your mind to expect the best possible outcome

Part of loving yourself is allowing yourself to be optimistic even in the worst possible situations. Much of the challenges we go through in life could be much easier if we adopted the right mindset while going through them. It's not easy to look up when you feel stuck in the mud, but mastering the art of resilience and thinking about what you have learned from that particular situation.

4. Give yourself praise

Always remember to celebrate your wins however small they may seem in that particular moment. Your mind needs that reassurance and gratitude for a job well done, so make it more permanent by writing the feeling down in a gratitude journal. Compliment yourself even when you lose because you're teaching your body that it is okay, even if things don't work out.

5. Be open to receiving love

Accept to receive love from other people so that you can learn to give it to other people when they need it the most. Many of us have been raised to mask raw emotion because when we previously dared to express how we truly felt, it was considered as a sign of weakness. The reality is we can never learn how to love others without realizing that we are also worthy of receiving love.

Uprooting Childhood Traumas

The word trauma is often used to signify a clear immensity of pain derived from a particular event in the past. It is often made to seem like for an event to be defined as traumatic, the victim must have experienced a direct brutal event, but what about the subtle trauma that is never defined? We all grow up believing that our childhoods were the best part of our lives, some people only realize later in life that certain experiences seem a little blurry than what actually happened. Those little unclear memories that keep slipping in and out of memory can turn out to be micro forms of trauma.

Subtle trauma can happen over a long period of time without the victim realizing that what is being done to them is wrong.

According to psychologist Margaret Crastnopol, subtle trauma can manifest in forms of actions that may seem insignificant in the moment but turn out to affect the victim in the long run (Nguyen, 2020). In a world where attention is only given to defined forms of trauma, victims of subtle trauma might find it confusing to uproot these feelings and embark on a healing journey. For instance, a person who was raised in a household where they were always punished for making slight mistakes might grow up to become defensive when confronted about their bad behavior. Certain forms of childhood trauma can include the following:

1. emotional gaslighting
2. abandonment
3. unfair punishment
4. sexual and physical abuse
5. loss of a parent

We all process trauma differently, which is why there is no one shoe-fits-all solution to heal from any of the different forms of trauma. Years of bottling up different kinds of trauma can create a mental block where the victim develops difficulty with creating healthy relationships with people. Childhood trauma can render a person unable to love others because they were never taught what it means to love themselves in the right way.

In order to overcome childhood trauma, you need to first identify the patterns that trigger you when you're feeling overwhelmed. Speaking to a trusted friend, the best way to overpower strong emotion is by letting it flow out of your body, allowing someone else to have access to your secret universe. Chances are you will get some form of reassurance and even if you may not appreciate advice from a person who you feel is not qualified to give advice about something they have never been through. But the benefit of that interaction is that it will sound less foreign to you, you will come to terms with the fact that you're a victim that needs to try to heal from the events of the past.

Trauma is repetitive, it will often be evident in your relationships, for instance, people that grew up in toxic homes will most often date people that remind them of that toxicity because the trauma remains unresolved. Some people are lucky to have access to therapy very early in their lives which can help them learn to live with their trauma in a healthy way. But not everyone can afford therapy, for a typical reader, you need to devise cheaper means of finding help. Learn to communicate with your body and listen to what it needs, while some people are comfortable sharing their trauma, others are more comfortable writing it down in a private journal. When you seek help, do not feel obliged to share your trauma when your mind is still trying to heal, be calm and let your body speak to you.

Knowing Your Triggers

To be triggered means to be reminded of a traumatic incident that happened in the past and getting the feeling that you are re-experiencing the trauma in that particular moment. Identifying your triggers requires that a person notices patterns in their behavior. It can be how you respond when your partner communicates how they feel, do you instantly become defensive or do you allow them to feel entitled to the way they feel? Another scenario can be an incident at your workplace where your subordinate shares a few tips on how you can be a better manager. Do you suddenly feel judged or do you take positive criticism kindly without letting your ego get in the way?

Some practical ways in which a person can learn to notice when they are about to be triggered is by taking five seconds to reflect before reacting in a heated situation. For instance, learning to set healthy boundaries at work, home, and in your normal day-to-day life. A healthy boundary at work can take the form of declining to take on an extra shift when experiencing burnout. We live in a society that prioritizes work culture more than rest days. In the middle of the grind culture, we easily lose connection with our reality in that we end up lashing out at loved ones and acting out of emotions.

The Bible has various examples of how Jesus withdrew from the crowd whenever he felt overwhelmed. In John 11:35, we are shown the vulnerable side of Jesus when he wept. On so many occasions Jesus restrained Himself from speaking in anger, He would pray to His Father to grant Him guidance to speak in love. There are very few incidents in the New Testament where Jesus loses His temper, for instance, when He found money lenders selling stuff in God's temple. He was so angry that He turned the tables upside down in the heat of the moment, it was clear that they had crossed His boundaries. So often we find ourselves in situations where we react out of anger when people we love cross our boundaries.

Being triggered should not be viewed with a negative connotation, it is merely a sign that someone has acted in a way that violates your personal values and beliefs. The truth is some of these beliefs may be based on unresolved trauma which is why everyone needs to keep note of those situations when they go off the radar. Those are the unresolved issues that need to be fixed in order to improve your relationships with other people.

Falling in Love With Your Flaws

The world is always quick to point out a person's flaws before they complement them on their positive attributes. While it is important to remain optimistic and focus on your positive traits, it is equally important to know your character flaws because it is the only way you're ever going to fix them. There is beauty in being flawed, it shows that you are part of the human experience. No one is perfect, therefore, the unfair standards we try to live up to are only fictional. Part of knowing yourself is learning to acknowledge your flaws and knowing that these flaws are not a weakness, they are unique to each individual. They tell a story of being open to unlearning toxic habits and relearning to associate with other people.

The Bible says that God's grace is made perfect in our weaknesses and that when we are at our weakest, God's love is made perfect (2 Corinthians 12:9 ESV) God doesn't expect us to be perfect, He created us in His own image and knows that we often fall short of His glory. He does not hold it against us because He has given us free will to make decisions on our own. God trusts that despite our flawed nature, we have the capacity to honor His word and live in accordance with His commandments. A lot of people in the Bible were flawed, God used these flawed people to preach the message of the gospel because He came to save the weak.

The relationship between Hosea and Gomer is a reflection of God's love for humankind regardless of our inherent sinful nature. God used Hosea to represent His love for Israel (represented by Gomer), Hosea who was a man of God was tasked to collect his wife-to-be Gomer from the brothels where she was working as a prostitute. Hosea is said to have paid over 15 pieces of silver for his wife, Gomer. This was in spite of the fact that by the standards of her life, society deemed her to be cheap, to be of less value compared to the women that had remained virgins until marriage. In a society that judged a man by the type of woman he married, where the sacredness of marriage was attributed to the woman's abstinence, Hosea chose to follow God's instructions. He loved Gomer even when she was unfaithful to him, he lovingly searched for her inside brothels and never once rubbed her sins in her face.

Hosea represents God's love for humankind, Gomer represents every one of us that is on the receiving end of God's love. This is how God expects us to love the people who are undeserving of love, because they need it the most. Because of Hosea's kindness and unconditional love, Gomer was able to give up her sinful life and live a life serving God. Just like Hosea, we should not use other people's weaknesses as leverage for our selfish endeavors. We should instead shower them with loving kindness so that they are able to see the power of God's love through us. This chapter has been extensive because we all needed to hold the mirror to ourselves, to find out where we stand in society when it comes to the definition of love. To discover what our understanding of love is and what is currently inhibiting us from loving other people the way God loves us. Take some time to find the answers to all that we have discussed.

Practical Exercise

1. What is the best way you can work on cultivating self-love?
2. Make a list of things you believe that you need to work on as a person in order to love yourself better.
3. Notice the situations that always drive you out of your normal temperament. Those are your triggers that you need to work on. Notice the patterns and work on them.
4. What are some childhood beliefs that you have had to unlearn?
5. Write down a list of things you have learned about yourself from this chapter.

Chapter 2:

Molding Your Relationship With God

The world is quick to associate any topic related to religion as limited to people that have fully dedicated themselves to serving God, as if sinners have no place in the presence of God. This is ironic given the fact that the entire teaching of the Bible is based on the fact that God is love. His love is sufficient for us, it is not limited to the people that society deems to be the great. The Bible itself calls upon "all" those who are heavy laden and that God will give them rest, it does not say "come you perfect people," God's invite is open to everyone that is going through challenges.

This is why it is important that each of us have the opportunity to meet with God during our weakest times because when we meet God with a vulnerable and pure heart, He listens to prayers of our hearts. The term "God" connotes a higher power, something that is omniscient and everlasting, which is why people are so often scared of the idea that they can commune directly with such a Divine Being. The great news is that God knew that mankind would experience that initial disconnect, which is why He sent His only son to earth to represent the human side of God and remind us all that we are one with God.

Who is your God? What comes to your mind when someone says that you need to have a personal relationship with God? There are several religions that exist in our society, so much so that so many people are confused. They want to be associated with a particular religious denomination that it blinds the fact that the most important aspect of spirituality is developing a personal relationship with God. This is regardless of whether you identify as a Christian, Atheist, Muslim, or Buddhist to mention but a few. A relationship should be personal, it should be a safe place where you go when you need to feel heard. If religion is such a strong concept for you, try to imagine a relationship with God as that which you have with a close friend of yours.

God means different things to different people, but in this context, God is the power that we serve, He is that still small voice we hear when we are all alone, and the voice that gives us hope when we feel let down by the world. God holds the answers to all that is unknown to a human mind, to be able to understand our existence we need to patiently study His word, and allow the Holy Spirit to reveal God's likeness to us. God is not some deity that is waiting to strike us down when we make a mistake, He has been personified in human form when He sent His only son, Jesus, to die for our sins. He knows what it feels like to be in the human body.

God experienced everything that we experience as humans. He was sent to the desert for 40 days and was tempted by Satan, He resisted temptation, and stuck to fulfilling His purpose on earth. God was betrayed by His disciple, Simon, He was sentenced to death for a sin He did not commit, and He had the power to just say well, "I am holy and do as I say," but He retained His form in the body of His son, Jesus Christ. He was made to carry a crown of thorns and beaten by the pharisee, every single thing that we experience in life, God has been through that as well. He wants us to know that we share the same body with Him.

Communing With God

Although God is a higher power, He has given us the gift of free will. He will never force us to be part of His Kingdom because He wants genuine hearts and souls. Because of our free will, we have the power to sin or refrain from sinning, all He can do is guide us through His word. God expects us to be able to declare that we serve Him and to inform all other people. He wants to be sure that whoever is seeking Him is seeking Him with a pure heart.

Sometimes it will be harder for you to communicate with God especially when you're going through tough times, the Devil whispers louder and wants you to believe that your belief in God is unfounded. But it is during those tough times that we need to be closer to God because He is busy molding our personalities to learn to stand through those periods of scarcity.

For those people that are hearing about the concept of God for the first time, your first steps to developing this relationship will be picking a time to study the Bible. The best way to know God is by reading about Him, not in the serious way that you do a factual study about the Bible stories and whether they make sense after more than a thousand years of being written. Do it in a way of feeding your curiosity, allow your mind to explore the possibility that there is a power higher than all of us that is all-knowing and is the reason for our entire existence.

Start with talking to God in the middle of your day, it could be a short conversation while you're stuck in the middle of traffic or while you complete your morning run. The trick is to make it so normal to whisper short requests like "God, please help me get to work on time" or "God, help me get through this day without being rude to anyone." While sometimes the conversation might need to be tougher than a simple sentence, set an hour aside for quiet time where you reflect on your life and sit still without any interruptions. While seated in silence, make a list of the questions you would like to ask God if you were given an opportunity to sit right in front of Him, and listen for the still small voice. God desires to listen to all the things that are happening in your life whether good or bad, and when you remain patient, you will understand how His Kingdom works.

Although this section preaches the importance of that personal relationship with God, it might be surprising for some of you to find out that that relationship even gets better when you learn in fellowship with other believers. A journey shared with others is one worth taking because when you're going through your season of weakness, the other people from your fellowship might be in their season of strength. The Bible itself says that iron sharpens iron, so one person sharpens another (Proverbs 27:17 ESV). Therefore, join a group of people that are on the same spiritual journey as you are, and from listening to their testimonies, you will have a broader understanding of the power of God. You will also learn how to love people during their times of need, the world has not taught us how to treat each other with compassion, and maybe you haven't seen these examples in the place you grew up.

Demystifying the Myth of God

It is easy for people without a spiritual background to believe that God is the mystical creature that only exists inside the walls of the church. To make matters worse, some religious leaders have made it seem that they hold the keys to access God. They request believers to approach them whenever they need to speak to God, which would be okay if only they preached about the importance of each believer developing a personal relationship with God. God is much more than who your preacher tells you about on a Sunday morning, and your spirituality should not be limited to the two to three hours you spend at church.

Your relationship with God should be treated like any other friendship and like any relationship you need to invest time, have intimate conversation, and share activities together. Best friends have deep conversations but when they don't spend time together, they grow apart and very often lose contact with each other. When we ignore God's word, we lose track of the direction and counsel, which is written in the Bible. The next question you must be asking yourself is "What part of the Bible should I read in order to learn more about God?" The Bible is not like any other book where you read from the beginning to the end, you need to understand.

God created Adam and Eve in order to commune with them in the garden of Eden, therefore, it was so sad when Eve disobeyed God by eating the forbidden fruit. Because of their disobedience, their relationship with God became distant, they felt too unclean to approach God. The way the Bible was written is a beautiful narrative of God trying to win back His friendship with man. He pursues us like how a man goes after a woman he is interested in, although God's love is much more pure.

There are a lot of false beliefs that certain religions keep spreading about the workings of God, which is why God is still portrayed as this unreachable being that is so foreign. Different religious belief means that there are several restrictions and, sometimes the government itself, imposes unfair laws on religious practices. According to the Pew Research Center, the social restrictions imposed on religious groups were higher in Muslim countries like Syria and Iraq (Baronavski et al., 2021).

Discovering God's Plan for Your Life

We were all created and placed on earth for a very specific reason. In Jeremiah 29:11 (ESV), He strongly declares that He knows the plans He holds for each and every one of His believers. God promises us plans of prosperity and a beautiful future, but we always forget to finish the rest of the chapter. God desires that we serve Him while on earth in return for the beautiful reward he holds for us in Heaven. In order to be aligned with God's plan, we need to offer certain aspects of ourselves:

1. Time

    God wants to get to know us as much as we want to get to know Him. It might sound odd that the person who created us would want to get to know us, but yes, once we are placed on earth, we become slaves to our human needs and that is why we dedicate ourselves to God through baptism. The concept of time in the Bible is relevant, He says we should commune with Him every day of our lives in order to know what He has in store for us. Today, spending time with God means attending church every time you are able to, serving in church and also offering to the church in order to build it.

2. Conversation

A lifetime of service to the Lord means you have the freedom to ask Him about anything without feeling like you are speaking to someone much more ordained than you are. God wants us to be His friends, He wants us to tell Him about our days the way we would tell our best friends. God speaks to us through various ways, He can send messages through our fellow believers and can also send them through the Bible itself. Every believer needs to be willing to listen to God's answers when we ask Him for clarity.

3. Commitment

There are only two worlds, the world of God's people and that of those who serve the Devil. None of us can serve two masters at once. This means that one cannot claim to be God's servant today and then go serve the Devil tomorrow. When we dedicate ourselves to God, He desires that we remain loyal to the kingdom and He also makes it clear that the consequences of sin is punishment. Wait on God to reveal His plan to you, pray and fast about your family, finances, and career whenever you feel stuck, ask God to show you the way.

It is important to reiterate that God's promises are pure, the Bible says in Genesis 17:16 (ESV) His promises are like silver which has been refined seven times, which means we can always rely on Him even when the Devil whispers words of discouragement during our trying time. For instance, Sarah was barren her whole life, she prayed to God for a child and God promised to bless her womb. Sarah waited for so long that she only became pregnant at the age of 99, giving birth to her son, named Isaac, who served the Lord for the rest of his life. I can imagine what mockery people made out of Abraham and Sarah as they waited to conceive at such an old age, and God came to prove Himself once again.

Practical Exercise

1. What does God mean to you?
2. Write down what comes to your mind when you commune with God.
3. What misconceptions have you heard about God that you have come to disprove?
4. Make a note of the times you felt like you heard God's voice. What did the voice sound like to you? What do you need to do to gain closeness with God?
5. What can you do today that will help make your relationship with God better?

Chapter 3:

Becoming One With the Universe

The heavens declare the glory of God; the skies proclaim the work of his hands. Day after day they pour forth speech; night after night they display knowledge. There is no speech or language where their voice is not heard. —Psalms 19:1 ESV

We were born into this world to exist for a certain period of time before God calls us back, which means we are always living on borrowed time. No one knows the time and place when God will come back and take His faithful servants with Him to heaven. We exist in a universe that consists of 8 planets, 7 continents, 195 countries with over 7,100 languages worldwide. The universe is diverse and according to the world bank, there are over 7,753 billion people living on planet Earth (Data Commons, n.d.). The world is ever-evolving. Once upon a time between 200,000 and 50,000 years ago, humans used the Proto-Human language to communicate and as the years went by modern languages were created. That is why we are able to read books like these, to translate messages into several different languages, learn about ancient cultures, and live harmoniously in our communities.

So, where does an individual fit into this huge picture called the Universe? What happens to our human bodies as we grow from being babies to toddlers and finally into fully grown adults? Why were we put on this planet? Couldn't God have taken us with Him to heaven immediately after the creation story? What is the point of living when the end goal is to die? These are the questions that often go through our minds as we get to understand the immensity of being human, and as we navigate through the challenges life throws at us, it is easy to experience an existential crisis. One of the ways the human mind can scale down the immensity of this existence is by learning to be still, listening to small signs that the Universe throws at us and learning to be patient with fellow human beings because we're all going through a human experience.

So many people have failed to make a link between the Universe and their religious journey, these days we find ourselves thanking the universe when something good happens. People find themselves asking the Universe to be kind to them and surrendering their fate to what the Universe holds for them. What some people fail to understand is that God is the Universe, He created it in a period of six days and rested on the seventh day. He is the beginning and the end, He is the air that we breathe, He gives life, and takes it away as He pleases. God is at the center of everything, when God created the Heavens, he wanted to show humankind the glory of His name, the Universe is a manifestation that we serve a living God.

We all exist in a world so diverse that we have somehow come to believe that we experience life the same way, which is a paradox of its own because there is some truth to the fact that the human experience is strangely similar for everyone. However, when a person focuses on the smaller details, our lives are in fact completely different because we have all been put on earth on our own journey. Yes, the families we are born into determine our first acceptance into society, but at a certain point each and every one of us has reached a point where they wanted more than just belonging to a family. Some call it searching for your true purpose, while others believe that by surrendering to the Universe, they can receive direction on how to become the best versions of themselves through practicing mindfulness.

The easiest way to know where you fit into that big puzzle of existence is by allowing your soul to find connection with the Universe. This chapter will highlight the different ways we can practice mindfulness in order to be aligned with the Universe, which reflects God's will. The key is to learn to look beyond our physical differences, the color of our skin, and the weakness in our human nature. The Universe is always guiding us but we cannot be guided if we are busy pursuing worldly pleasures, and we cannot live in harmony with others if we are not at peace within ourselves. Only until we learn to accept that our differences are what makes us unique, and that we need to celebrate and embrace them to make us part of the big family of life, we shall never find inner peace as we live.

A perfect example of this is the book *The Alchemist* by Paulo Coelho about a young boy named Santiago who has a dream of finding hidden treasure. In his dream, he gets a vision that his treasure is under the pyramids in Egypt and embarks on a journey to find that treasure, during which he finds a lot of people that mentor him, direct him towards his purpose. A few of these people actually stole from him and set him back from his goal, he could have lost track of his goal but he persisted through the challenges. He allowed his soul to be immersed into the universe, he treated every single omen that the universe revealed to him as an important part of his journey.

At the end of his journey, to a human mind he seems like he has lost more than gained, because his treasure was stolen twice and he did not even find anything under the pyramids. But to a spiritual person, Santiago lost the world and gained himself, i.e. his experiences let him shade the naivety of existence, he fell in love with Fatimah, and therefore, had a bigger goal to achieve after leaving Egypt. He also learned the importance of surrendering to the power of the Universe because he followed all the signs the Universe gave him. By doing so, he was able to find out the actual location of the treasure was around his hometown (1993).

Consciousness

The human mind is the most complex feature of our physical bodies, it consists of the conscious mind when we are awake and the unconscious state when we are asleep. To simply define consciousness, it is the awareness of ourselves and our environments. According to an American psychologist named William James, consciousness is a constant stream of energy between the mind and the body (Harvard's Psychology Department, 2022). James believed that our emotions are caused by our response to external stimuli and, therefore, our internal states have a direct relation to external circumstances in our environment.

Our human attention span keeps changing, one moment we are reading a book and when our toddlers come tagging, we might put that book aside and focus on something else. To connect with the Universe, we need to understand how our human brain works and how to train it to remain focused in times when we feel overwhelmed with emotion. Every person you meet has a certain energy that they give off. Notice how you act when you are around people that throw you off balance, learn how to protect your energy from people that are always giving off negative energy.

Our consciousness can be altered through various ways which include practicing mental exercises, through meditation, hypnosis, and taking medication to mention but a few. In the next subsection, we will delve into the different ways an individual can practice altering their conscious states in order to gain control over their emotions and feel better aligned with their environment.

Practicing Mindfulness

The idea of being mindful denotes learning to love in the present moment, learning to sit still, and letting your mind wander out of your body. Mindfulness exercises allow us to channel our unconscious emotions and interpret them before reacting to anything that is happening in our conscious state. We live in a stressful world where our emotions go through highs and lows within a short period of time, the lives that we lead often leave us so busy that we would rather use a quick fix like a cigarette, a quick energy drink, or a sleeping pill whenever our bodies signal stress, fatigue, or discomfort.

When we use quick destructive methods to fix temporary emotions of stress, we alter our brain's thought process of interpreting emotions. Our body consists of the nervous system which regulates how the body interprets messages from the outside world when we are in a scary situation our emotions are heightened and a part of our brains, called the amygdala, immediately sends a message to the hypothalamus which sends a signal to the nervous system. Our nervous system then releases the hormone called adrenaline which causes an increase in the heart rate and often causes us to sweat. In this split second, a person decides whether they need to fight the danger to run away (flee) from the danger (Harvard Health Publishing, 2020).

When a person is stressed, the human body goes through a thousand neural responses before the person reacts, therefore, in that split second, we react in an automated mode. Most of the time this reaction is irrational and based on pure emotion, that is why the constant trigger of the stress hormone when we are experiencing short-term inconveniences like maybe running late for work, dealing with a flat tire, or even just the thought of engaging in social activities can cause chronic stress.

This is where the importance of mindfulness comes in, when we learn to be still even in moments that call for flight, we teach our bodies to react rationally in situations that are seemingly out of our control. If you have ever heard someone narrate an incident where they had to swerve away from ongoing traffic in a dangerous situation, they will often say something like "I don't know what happened, I just swerved to the left and missed the cyclist by an inch." This is because the human brain has processed the danger in split seconds and for a mindful person, they will unconsciously choose the best viable option for survival. Here are some of the ways you can tune into your surroundings by practicing mindfulness, some of the activities may take a while to become a habit but what matters is daily practice:

1. Meditation

   Many of us are so scared of listening to the tune of our emotions because we have been accustomed to building this mental block whenever faced with intense emotions. Meditation is the act of quieting your mind in order to connect to your innermost thoughts in the mind, which are basically the core of your soul. When some people think of meditation, they imagine the beautiful magazine pictures of women seated cross-legged at a tropical resort, breathing in and out the fresh air and this is a completely false representation of meditation. The essence of meditation is to allow your mind to think so big and yet your body is acting so little. In essence, yes, you can mentally travel to that tropical beach, but you do not have to be in the perfect location to meditate. The trick is to learn to do it amid the stress, during that awkward conversation with a loved one, or yet, in the midst of that hectic work day where everything seems to be falling apart. Here is an example of a meditation technique that I have learned to use.

Exercise 1:

Look around the room you're seated in right now as you read this book. Let your mind focus on the item that brings you the most peace, it could be the beautiful potted plant on your windowsill. Notice how green the leaves are, turn your attention to the vase that holds the plant, the pattern on the vase, and how it intricately holds the life of the plant. Let this focus go on for about 15 minutes. Notice how your mind is completely focused on the growth of the potted plant that you haven't thought about before, rather than what was initially stressing you out. Your mind will be reconnected to your body so that you are in a state of awareness that the stressful situation is only 5% of your life at that particular moment.

According to spiritual teacher Deepak Chopra, when we meditate to relieve stress, we become healthier both mentally and emotionally and as we turn into the habit of meditating even without the need to release stress, we learn deeper aspects about our humanity (Oprah Winfrey Network, n.d.). We become more connected to other people and develop feelings of loving-kindness to other people because we realize that the universe is our source of connection.

2. Yoga

Traditional yogis believe that if you can control your breathing, you can control your mind, when you control your breathing, you can control your feelings. Once again, there are a lot of myths about yoga. Yoga is different from meditation because while meditation focuses on strengthening the mind, yoga works on both physical and mental agility. According to The Yoga Institute, many people have been deceived by mainstream media that yoga is about fancy poses when it is really deeper than that. Yoga is a way of life, it is a way of connecting our subconscious minds to the power of the Universe, to be able to travel through dimensions that our normal conscious state would not be able to do (The Yoga Institute, 2018).

Yoga has different levels; it is important to know where you stand before you begin practicing yoga. Teach yourself about the origins of yoga, then develop an independent mindset about what you hope to attain from the practice. The benefits of yoga are so diverse because it deals with the inner workings of the spirit. Although traditionally, yoga was associated with the Sanskrit traditions, it has evolved in the modern world and received recognition from health professionals. It is now more than a spiritual experience. Studies by the American College of Physicians have shown that medical professionals now recommend yoga as the first stage of treatment for chronic lower back pain and neck pain (National Center for Complementary and Integrative Health, 2019).

The beauty of yoga is the fact that it connects us as humans, we learn to manage our mental health issues, deal with past trauma and heal in ways that we do not project our fears on others. If you notice, some people immediately become kinder and at peace when they practice yoga. While this may not be the outcome for everyone, our bodies react differently to certain practices therefore the key is to try everything until you find your niche.

Exercise 2:

Yoga begins as a personal journey, find an instructor that will guide you through the basic practices then once you advance to a level where you can do it on your own, make space for your yoga sessions at home. That space should remain your sacred sanctuary that you go to when you need to be still and listen to what the universe wants to tell you.

3. Physical Exercises

The body is the vessel that carries our entire existence, without it there are no emotions, there is no mind to work on and no existence at all. This is why it is important to always give it our utmost attention when practicing mindfulness. When we don't take care of our bodies, we not only develop health issues like high blood pressure, obesity, diabetes and all other ailments that arise from physical inactivity, but also, we open a door for mental challenges like depression, anxiety, and low self-esteem to mention but a few. Once again when our perspective of the self-diminishes, we react by lashing out at other people, and it ends up affecting the way we love other people.

Physical exercise can draw us closer to the universe because when we exercise, our bodies release endorphins that help us to relieve stress. It also matters where the physical exercise takes place, while some people might prefer to exercise indoors, there are proven benefits of exercising outside and being able to interact with nature while you do it. According to Mihaly Csikszentmihalyi, a Hungarian-American psychologist, human beings are capable of achieving a state of happiness when they concentrate on activity so much that they gain a high level of productivity, he refers to this as the "state of flow." We can achieve this state of flow by incorporating it into our exercise routine (Marder, 2022).

Exercise 3:

The best way to be mindful of our bodies is to engage in mindful physical exercises in our daily routine. This means that when you set out for your morning walk, do not only focus on the fact that you want to reach that particular goal weight. Focus rather on the movement of your body, notice how your legs move one in front of the other, remind yourself that just like walking, some days even the act of putting one leg in front of the other will be enough. This will remind you that good things are a result of small efforts which are repeated even on those days when you do not feel like it.

Living in the Moment

When we learn to take each day as it comes, we are teaching ourselves to constantly live in a state of calm. Then, through this clear state, we are able to manifest the things that we dream about. According to Echakrt Tolle, when a person is not present in the moment, you will struggle to obtain the intuition that guides you where your intellect cannot (Oprah Winfrey Network, n.d.). He also emphasizes that when we operate in consciousness awareness, we avoid making decisions out of our ego, or intellect.

- Learning to live in the moment, being conscious, and allowing the Universe to speak to us.
- Allowing nature to be part of our human experience. Communing with Nature.
- The power of "I am."
- Acknowledging our entire human experience, allowing ourselves to make mistakes, and learning from them.
- The bliss of taking a nature walk.
- Breathing. You're always one breath away from choosing how you respond to the world. Mantras that help to live in the now (Oprah Winfrey Network, n.d.).

Practical Exercise

1. How do you practice your self-care when you need to find balance in your life?
2. Describe what your human existence means to you. Try to create a picture of your role in the Universe.
3. What type of personality do you have? Reflect on how your personality affects the way you relate to people. Think about which method of connection would work best for you as either an introvert or extrovert.
4. Write about the last time you felt really present. What decision would you make today that would help you regain that feeling?
5. What techniques of mindfulness have you used before to help with your anxiety? How did they help you cope with your anxiety?

Chapter 4:

Solo Spiritual Journey

At the beginning of this book, we discussed the connection between our mind, body, and spirit. We have also established that spirituality and religion are a huge part of our human existence, now, this chapter will delve into the benefits of embarking on a solo spiritual journey. We have all been at that point in life where we felt a little disconnected from everything, whether it is a job, being a parent, engaging with family members, etc. and have reached that point of questioning our belief systems.

In the Bible, when God wanted to ordain people as priests, they would embark on spiritual journeys for purification. The Catholic and Muslim religions still practice pilgrimage during Lent season and Ramadan respectively. God, Himself, resorted to the desert for 40 days when He needed to prepare to fulfill His purpose. He had to be tested by the Devil in the desert, He went 40 days without food, and only lived by the gospel. It was through these testing times that He was able to withstand hate from Pilate and his men, that He preached His Father's word to the gentiles, and ushered countless numbers of people back to Christ. God expects all of us to emulate the example of His Son, to learn to sacrifice our comfort, strip ourselves from the chains of worldly pleasures, and stand before Him offering our souls for the service of His Kingdom.

The idea of a spiritual journey has evolved over the years, you do not need to travel and spend 40 days in a desert to discover the spirituality that is aligned with your lifestyle. The essence of a spiritual journey is to allow your mind to discover new versions of God. You have accomplished the first step of getting to know who you are, therefore, this step of discovering your highest level of spirituality should be a breeze. Pray every day to your Higher Power, some people pray to

God, some people find spiritual leaders to guide them through prayer, other people prefer to read literary works, and most of us basically just Google answers or watch YouTube. Whatever information you get from these sources, pray about it, and ask God to help you discern what is right from wrong.

At the core of all our upbringing is a set of core values that you live by, these values can help guide you on who to approach to mentor you on your journey. God has given us the spirit of discernment, do not let the fear of discovering the unknown stop you from exploring your true spiritual self. Use your mindfulness journey to allow you to awaken your mind to be accepting of answers that are way out of your normal field of access. To be elevated will require another level of yourself, which means you will have to change certain aspects of your life. You have to be sure of the things that you allow to access your energy, for instance, the television shows you allow your mind to watch, the type of food you let into your body, and the kind of people you allow yourself to engage with. People can either speak life into you or drain the life out of you.

The whole reason for embarking on a spiritual journey is to search for answers to certain life questions. Some people embark on a journey when dealing with the loss of a loved one. Grief can be a great motivator in such circumstances because the person would want to figure out the meaning of life. The Universe will always have clear answers when a person shows up in a vulnerable state, it is during these times that our minds are committed to searching for the meaning of our existence. Another reason may be the search for healing from traumatic religious activities, for instance, a person whose entire life has been defined through the confines of the church they belong to may struggle with forming independent opinions for themselves, and they could feel trapped in a system that has existed longer than their lifetime.

It is okay to question beliefs that no longer fit into the puzzle of your life, in Jeremiah 29:13 (ESV), God, in fact, encourages us to ask questions in order to get answers. He states that when we search for Him with pure hearts, we will find Him. He desires a pure heart with the intention of really getting to understand how the Kingdom of God works. He does not expect us to follow blindly like blind sheep, His desire is that we learn to love Him the way He loves us. Until a person discovers the true love of God and breaks the ungrounded foundations of their belief system to be rooted in God, they will never learn how to give love to someone that is so undeserving of it. God does not expect us to keep company with people who drain us of our need to love, however, He does expect us to show them love. It is challenging to know where to draw the line when it comes to associating with people whose energy does not vibrate at the level of your own, but through prayer, we can all learn to love them, even if it means loving them from a distance.

Religious Denominations

There are several forms of spirituality that the world has been exposed to, and while this may seem good, it can be confusing to figure out which one is aligned with a person's values. Therefore, this section will highlight how to find your spiritual journey and choose which religion to align with your spirituality. There is a vast majority of religious affiliations that exist in the world today, you have probably heard about them before, therefore, I will only briefly describe why there are several branches of Christianity today. Jesus' ministry started all the way from the period called the A.D "After Christ," and different religious sects developed because of geographical locations and culture. In the beginning, the Christian church operated as one and it was only in 1,054 A.D that the Christians split from the Catholics. They disagreed on certain sacraments and also beliefs. For instance, the Catholics believed in absolution through a priest while the Protestants believed in direct communication with God (Coffey, 2021).

There is a vast majority of differences that caused the division but without going into too much detail, the core of the division was practical differences. It is important for every believer to realize that at the core of our spirituality is the belief in the Higher Power, Muslims call their god Allah, the Baha'is refer to God as 'Dios', the Buddhists refer to God as Buddha, and the Hindu people have several names for their gods and goddesses. There is no standard measure of which religion is better than which, however, you can use a pedestal by weighing in which religion makes you feel more at home. Here are a few tips that can help you find the right church:

1. A religion that teaches hatred or judgment towards people that are considered unworthy should immediately be a red flag. There are some religious practices that are still completely based on Old Testament teachings like the idea of an "eye for an eye" which the Israelites used in the old times when they lived according to the law of retribution. The New Testament preaches the gospel of forgiveness and calls for Christians to let God do the punishing for them. It is basic humanity to know that one cannot get justice through revenge, therefore, if any of the spiritual gatherings you attend encourage this type of behavior, leave immediately.

2. Be aware of churches or religious gatherings that preach the prosperity gospel. The reality of life is that it comes with challenges, there will never be a permanent guarantee of everything being perfect. Instead, choose a religion that teaches you how to navigate through the changing times of life and how you can maintain patience in an ever-changing world. Yes, God promises to reward His faithful servants according to His riches in glory. This doesn't mean that every one of us gets to be financially liberated during our earthly stay. Riches in the Bible refer to being blessed with spiritual food like the gift of love, joy, patience, peace and abundance, but not the money we think of.

3. Our bodies speak to us after every church or spiritual event we attend. Listen to your spirit immediately after attending church. It can only be either you feel hopeful, relaxed, and patiently waiting for your season, or you feel completely judged and like

you're undeserving of the love of God. If you struggle to listen to your soul, try some of the mindful exercises that we discussed in the previous chapter, be still and listen!
4. Disassociating yourself from the narrative of religion without losing your touch with the basic teachings of religious texts. So many feel more comfortable being part of a group of believers, such people might feel more at home being part of organized religion. However, for an individual who has been raised in a strict religious home, they might have questions about exploring other religions without the fear of being judged. It is also possible for them to embark on a spiritual journey that is not specifically associated with the conventional regions. It can be tricky to navigate the non-conventional religious journeys because not many people are open-minded enough to understand why you would visit a Sharma, a palm reader, astrologist, or spiritual leader. First, read about the history of each, understand the core of their beliefs, then you may either leave it at that or use it to supplement your own religious values.

Discovering Your Spiritual Preference

There is spirituality you're born into then there's the one you discover for yourself. The one that lets you believe that, regardless of your shortcomings, you're always going to feel loved. For you to attain a high vibration of spiritual maturity, you need to be able to put God out of the box that society has placed Him in. That is, you need to realize that regardless of your religious affiliation, your relationship with your God is all that matters. At the end of our lives, God will not ask under what religion you served Him, all He will want to know is whether you dedicated your life to serving Him and drawing more people to His Kingdom.

Just like your relationships with other people, you always need to find a way to nurture your spirituality. The best way Christians do this is by reading religious texts and applying them to their current circumstances. Elizabeth Gilbert is a celebrated author who wrote the book, *Eat, Pray, Love*. In the book, she talks about her struggle with depression during the time of her divorce. One particular night she finds herself seated on the floor of her bathroom crying out to God and asking Him what she could do to feel better, there, in the midst of her brokenness, she heard God say (2006):

> "Go back to bed," said the omniscient interior voice, "because you don't need to know the final answer right now, at three o'clock in the morning on Thursday in November. 'Go back to bed', because I love you. 'Go back to bed', because the only thing you need to do for now is get some rest and take good care of yourself until you do know the answer." —Elizabeth Gilbert, *Eat, Pray, Love: One Woman's Search for Everything Across Italy, India, and Indonesia*

Elizabeth had no idea how much God was about to reveal Himself to her over the years that followed. She took a solo pilgrimage through Italy, India, and Indonesia, and throughout that journey, she learned about various spiritual practices that could help her build a stronger relationship with God. She had to shade off her old skin, all her traumas from her previous relationships that came back to her, and continue on her journey. Even on those days where she felt like she needed to take the next flight back to what she considered home, her spiritual growth allowed her to overlook those temporary pleasures for the bigger picture at hand.

Communal Spirituality vs. Individual Spirituality

Knowing that you are stronger with others or stronger as an individual is an essential part of your spiritual journey. While traditional pilgrimages were usually done as solo travels, today people can take them as a group, or can also choose to do both the solo and group journey without feeling the pressure of choosing one over the other.

Here are some examples of spiritual practices that can teach you to relearn the core of love:

1. Connect with other like-minded people who are on the same journey as you are. Not only will this guide your journey, it will keep you balanced during those days that you have to set out alone. In the Bible, God calls us to fellowship with other believers in order to keep ourselves accountable to each other. Church fellowship might be the best way to start off your spiritual retreat, as you worship God together, you will be given an opportunity to.
2. Change your diet. It is true that we are what we eat and our bodies respond to whatever we feed them. Some people mistake spiritual diet for that of people that are fully vegetarian which is not true. A person should merely be mindful of the type of food that they eat. Without going into the details of processed versus plant-based food choices, just start by observing how your energy levels feel after eating a certain meal. The nutrients contained in food are broken down and are released into the body in the form of hormones, and each type of food contributes a different nutrient to the brain. It is important to maintain a balanced diet in order to maintain healthy brain function. When we eat foods high in sugar, they are broken down into glucose which flows into our blood system and high levels of glucose lead to low levels of energy.
3. Pray every day without ceasing

    Most people like to accompany their prayer with long periods of fasting. Fasting is the denying of oneself worldly pleasures for a specific period of time as one journeys with God. This means restricting yourself from worldly pleasures like food, sexual immorality, social media, and anything that will distract you from your communion with God. It is through prayer that God will guide you on whether you need to join other believers in prayer or continue on your solo journey. Prayer will also reveal what is unknown to a mere human mind because it is through faith that we believe in the existence of a higher power, this faith can be used to interpret spiritual teachings and help a person redefine their belief system to be in line with what God desires.

Practical Exercise

1. What event prompted you to take a spiritual journey?
2. What kind of environment best elevates your spiritual thoughts?
3. Challenge yourself to take long nature walks where you allow the universe to speak to you.
4. Start keeping a food journal, not to take note of the calories but merely to write down how your body feels after eating certain foods.
5. When it comes to spirituality, are you an absolutist or a non-absolutist? An absolutist is a person who only believes in the existence of one strict religion, while a non-absolutist is always open to learning new ideas about religion.
6. What is your personality type? Would you rather take a solo spiritual journey or a group retreat with other believers?
7. What religious denomination do you identify with? How do you feel about the concept of worshiping God without the limitations that religion provides?

Chapter 5:

Your Ego May Destroy You

The word ego is used when someone is focused more on protecting their sense of importance as compared to taking into consideration the other person's feelings. Merriam Webster describes the ego as the awareness of self in a person's conscious state of mind, basically being sure of one's self-esteem (n.d.). Every one of us has an ego, it's a natural-born trait of always trying to prove our sense of self-importance to others. This is normal if it is done moderately but can be dangerous if we let our egos run our lives. An inflated ego can ruin your relationships with the people you care about simply because you care so much to be right at the expense of other people.

There is an inner child inside every one of us, that child is always communicating something to us during those moments when we put our guards up and let our egos run us. Your inner child represents those unhealed parts of yourself that you continue to live with because you have never tried to do inner child work. If you're hearing about this term for the first time, buckle up! Your inner child is part of your subconscious mind that keeps a record of your first memories as a child, while you are still learning what is right from wrong. Our inner children remember if their emotions were always met with punishment, feelings of love that were never openly expressed, the fear of being punished for making a mess, and the fear of not belonging, to name a few.

Very few people have taken steps to work with their inner child, this means having active conversations with your five-year-old self and teaching them to unlearn some of the coping mechanisms that they had to use to survive then. According to a Swiss psychologist, Carl Gustav Jung, while our inner child might be childlike, carefree, non-judgmental, and curious to learn new stuff, that child can also carry emotional trauma from past abuse (My Online Therapy, 2021). The first step to re-parenting your inner child is realizing the incidents that trigger them to show themselves. It could be that whenever someone tries to correct you when you're wrong, you fear that once they establish your weakness, you're going to be mocked for not knowing how to do something. It could be your inability to admit when you have hurt someone's feelings because your inner child was never taught how to be held accountable for their actions.

Your inner child might always be seeking validation from others; therefore, it is one of the reasons some people develop an inflated ego. No one wants to associate with a person who always fronts their unhealed trauma through an inflated ego, you might not even notice you're doing it until you realize a pattern in your relationships–people always leave you. In order to develop long-lasting relationships with people, we need to learn to put our egos aside because sometimes an inflated ego can cause a person to act irrationally. This chapter will navigate ways a person can use their ego both for good and also do away with it if it injures their relationships.

Myths About Ego

Mainstream media has made people tune into this idea of nurturing their ego due to every celebrity talking about the principles of always putting themselves first. The younger generation is watching the adults nurse their egos at every given opportunity. It is the small acts like screaming at another driver during your commute because they failed to turn on their indicator light in time. That small act may seem insignificant to you, but your child is watching you. You're teaching your child to always try to show this sense of self-importance in situations that do not call for it.

However, there is a completely different side of ego that children need to be taught about: The fact that there are situations where your ego can be beneficial to you. Ego is how an individual values themselves in society. There are a lot of times when your children will need to learn how to stand up for themselves in situations of injustice. Build up your child's confidence so much that when they enroll in school and start interacting with other children, they can discern which fights to pick and which ones are not worth their time. There is a thin line between a strong healthy ego and a weak ego. The former allows us to recognize our strength during trying terms and also strengthens our relationships with others, while the latter causes us to act irrationally and do what feels comfortable in the moment.

Being Ego Driven vs. Purpose Driven

Our egos can be a serious motivation, but at what point should we realize our egos are being misleading and blocking us from having healthy relationships, and growing into and affecting other areas of our lives? An ego-driven person will strive to achieve a goal just to prove that they can do it better than the other people, while a purpose-driven person focuses on achieving the goal and teaching other people how they can also achieve the goal. A person who values validation from the external world will often feel demotivated when they achieve their goals and realize no one really cares. This can often lead to depression and feelings of wanting to over-inflate your level of self-importance in any given opportunity. It is from learning to be humble that we understand our achievements are ours to celebrate, and they do not make us any better than anybody else, we rarely become better versions of ourselves.

An ego-based mentality will most often keep your mind closed off from actual progress because the person's mind is so focused on short-term achievements instead of focusing on the picture of long-term achievements. Because the ego is self-serving, a person who follows their ego will rarely feel fulfilled. These are the people you will find trying to fit into different careers every year and never finding a permanent source of fulfillment.

When it comes to loving others, our egos can manifest when we attach conditions to our love, for example, telling your partner that you will only love them if they continue taking care of the bills at home. How many of us can say we have experienced true love throughout our entire lives? A love that is true, unconditional and always fulfilling is something that is very rare to find in this generation. We are so busy repressing our egos that we do not realize that authentic love when we find it in others because our trauma response makes us believe everyone is out to hurt us. There is a huge difference between ego love and authentic love, the former is self-seeking and does not nurture while the latter is fulfilling and often gives a person peace of mind.

How to Control Your Ego

We are all human, and sometimes, we get so deep into arguments that we do not realize when our egos are getting inflated. It is the reason you find a person yelling at a waitress in the restaurant for simply serving the eggs runny instead of hard like they had requested. Not accepting the fact that our human nature is prone to making mistakes and holding that pedestal so high when other people make mistakes is a sign of an inflated ego.

The Kentucky Counseling Center has laid out simple techniques of keeping your ego in check (2021):

1. The first step is knowing yourself. As we have already discussed at the beginning of Chapter One, when you take time to study your character you will be more forgiving towards your character flaws. The plus side is no one can use them against you because you know your weakness and are, hopefully, already working on becoming a better person. Knowing yourself means acknowledging that other people are not that different from you, and that everyone has traits that they need to work on in order to have better relationships with others.

2. Be rational. Allow your mind to think before you say anything that you might regret at a later stage. Our human instinct is to immediately engage in any argument that goes against our belief system, sometimes we let our emotions get in the way of reason and end up inflating our egos at the expense of learning something new. Ask yourself whether you have given the other person a chance to explain the reasoning behind their thought process before you force them to only consider your point of view.
3. Always take a minute to remind yourself that not everything should be taken personally. It is easy to assume that your opinion should always be the final point of departure in any given situation, and you might feel under looked when this does not happen. Remind yourself that other people coexist in the same environment and that they would also like to feel heard. This also means that you should be open to positive criticism. It's true, no one likes hearing someone tell them how to be a better parent or better work colleague. The first thought that comes to your mind shouldn't be that you're being singled out. Instead reflect on the feedback and ask them how you could have done better given those same circumstances.

According to Echkart Tolle, the best way to control your ego is to learn when to let the ego remain repressed in situations that do not require a reaction (Oprah Winfrey Network, n.d.). When someone steps on your toes, there's that automatic need to retaliate in order to defend your ego, but have you ever paused to ask yourself what would happen if you did not retaliate? By constantly practicing not pleasing our egos, we are teaching them that they do not hold power over us, therefore, we end up deflating them. There is a sense of power and control that develops every time you pick up on those moments when your ego has been hurt but your inner self does not feel the need to defend it, that is maturity.

Balancing Self-Love With Selflessness

We spoke about putting yourself entirely first without first considering how other people might feel about it, that is self-love and it takes years of practice to achieve a higher vibration of self-love. The concept of self-love is to teach yourself to put yourself first, but we have to be careful not to be so self-absorbed in that love that we forget to balance it out with helping other people when need be. The world we live in has emphasized the idea of self-love so much that we have not progressed to that stage after you love yourself so much that it overflows in order for other people to enjoy your love too.

No one is extending the message of learning to be selfless. What happens to all your self-love when you cannot help other people love themselves too? When it overflows so much that another person could use it how do you get on about making other people feel appreciated? Let's use a quick analogy here: The Holy Trinity is made up of God the Father, the Son, and the Holy Spirit. When God sent His Son to die for our sins, He literally sacrificed Himself for us. Think about that again, God loved Himself so much that He was willing to let His Son (part of Him) come to Earth and spread that message of love to His believers. Because of this great sacrifice, the enemy has no hold on us. We are forgiven even before we gather the courage to ask God for forgiveness.

It probably sounds a little too sacrificial, right? But God desires your heart that much, and this is how we should serve other people that really need that love. There is joy in giving, in sharing what you are blessed with. God will always remind us that all these things on earth will be worthless in Heaven, we are only custodians of God's riches, and He can take them back at any time that He desires. Every time we fail to help another person in need, we deny ourselves that joy that comes from knowing you don't have much but you have the willpower to make someone else happy by giving from the little you have.

Learning to be selfless does not mean denying yourself the pleasures of life, it means knowing that your riches will not be diminished just because you have shared a part of them. We have all heard the saying that time is money, the greatest gift you can give one another is time. By being selfless you're allowing yourself to share your time, share intangible things like mentoring a child that needs guidance, and using your talent to make other people happy. An important aspect of being selfless is that it helps to deflate your ego. That is if you're doing it with pure intentions with no need to announce to the world every time you do something selfless.

Practical Exercise

1. Do you believe you have an inner child within you? Think about the times that child speaks to you. At what age does your inner child show up as? Write about a significant event that happened to you on that particular date.
2. Keep an 'Ego Journal.' Write down all the times you have felt triggered to inflate your ego but have chosen to let it go instead.
3. What were you like during your childhood? Describe a time when you realized that the world was not as black and white as you thought.
4. Describe the first time you felt hurt by someone you loved.
5. Why do you think our ego always gets the best of us even when we try to suppress them?

Chapter 6:

Simple Acts of Love

The sole meaning of life is to serve humanity. –Leo Tolstoy

We have discussed so much about doing the inner work, but now, it is time we get to the practical side of this book. Think about the last time a random stranger showed you kindness. What were you doing, and how did it restore your faith in humanity? Sometimes we get so hooked on what is posted on social media that we forget the most genuine acts of love are not broadcasted on social media. Almost as if it isn't recorded then it did not happen.

Our first experience of love came from our parents. We learned how to be nice to our siblings, how to apologize when we are sorry, and how to share our snacks with others. As we keep growing, we become parents too and realize how unconditionally our children love us even when we tend to disappoint them. We would do anything to make sure that our children know that they are loved. Have you ever thought about showing this type of love to complete strangers? The type of love that ensures to leave the person feeling better than you found them? Because, as humans, we are all here to love others and to be loved by others. We need to look for the same love we give our family to random strangers.

This is how God expects us to show love to other people–to do it so much that it just happens out of habit. Simple acts of love are those small things we do when we are feeling generous. Sadly, this happens so rarely that when we do it we feel an outflow of energy that we've never felt before. So how can we make these acts so often that we no longer feel the need to let other people know what we did? Doing this is the only way to make this a habit. I'm going to try to use an analogy of the sun: The sun shines bright every day, even on some rainy days. It reaches each and every person on earth and brightens their mood. We all rely on the sun for light and for the growth of our plants. The sun's presence makes us feel warm and feeds our souls with love, regardless of how hard the day may seem, the sun will always show up the next day. Be someone's sun in their times of need, and be your own sun in times of your own need. Consider this balance.

My Brother's Keeper

The Bible talks about the fruits of the Holy Spirit: love, joy, peace, patience, kindness, goodness, faithfulness, gentleness, and self-control. These are the values that God wants us to live by as we relate to other people. The greatest of them all is love. This section will delve into a discussion of how we can practice biblical love in a world that is faced with so much hatred and bias.

The phrase of being your brother's keeper is derived from the book of Genesis from the story of Cain and Abel. When God asked Cain where his brother was, he responded sarcastically by saying, "I don't know. Am I my brother's keeper?" which was a really rhetorical sounding question when I read it. How many times do we feel like Cain? How many times are we so filled with our own selfish needs that we try to downplay the responsibility of being one another's keeper? The New Testament answers this question in Mark 12:31 where Jesus calls us to love our neighbors as we love ourselves, God expects us to keep an eye on each other and pick ourselves up when going through tough times.

The next question is, "Who is a neighbor?" Your neighbor isn't just the person living next to your family, the statement refers to every human being that you meet on Earth, they are your neighbor in that particular moment. Next question, "Would you be happy if your neighbor treated you the same way that you treat them?" If your answer is yes, then maybe my job here is done, but if you hesitated for a second then, work through the following list of how you can love your neighbor the way God requires us to:

1. Spend quality time with them.

   You're probably wondering how you're expected to spend time with a complete stranger without giving off an uncomfortable aura to them. The truth is, we spend most of our time behind our phone screens, sending sweet messages to check-in on people and this takes five seconds of your time. Because of modern technology, people no longer see the need to physically meet-up and have conversations about life and encourage each other. So your first task would be to find means of using your physical presence to show love to people that need it the most. For instance, find the nearest homeless center in your town and take a day off from work to go interact with the residents. Get to know their stories and offer them encouragement, read a book or two to them, and let them know that they still matter to the world. Stop doing the bare minimum by hiding behind your phone screen. There are therapeutic benefits people receive from the physical presence of kind strangers.

2. Show up when things go wrong.

   When you're woken up in the middle of the night to help a friend whose car has broken down in traffic, do not hesitate. Remind yourself that if they had other people they could rely on they would have called them, you might be someone's first and only option. There is a tendency to disappear from your friends when they seem to be struggling because society tells us that we are the company that we keep. This is a wrong mindset, your friends are people that rely on you for consolation during times of trouble, and are willing to give that energy back when they also need it.

3. If you are in a position of privilege, elevate other people with you.

   A lot of people are used to lending a listening ear to the problems of other people but doing nothing proactive about changing the situation at hand. What may seem like a small phone call to you might mean the world to someone else that needs that new job. Recommend the people you know that are in need of help, say their names in rooms that they cannot gain access to, be the vessel that they use to move from being nobody to becoming standing members of the society.

4. Give to charities that you feel passionate about.

This cannot be said enough, regardless of how much money you make; you can always be in a position to help people that are struggling to make ends meet. There are various numbers of charities ranging from homeless people, relief for victims of domestic violence, mental health awareness, the LGBTQ community, animal shelter, previously underprivileged communities, etc.

5. Be a mentor to the youth.

If you are an adult that has gone through various life experiences, use your story as a learning curve for the next generation. Volunteer at a high school, or in the local community, to give career guidance to the youth as they make their way into the challenging work environment. The Bible says that bad morals corrupt good company, be the voice of reason to these children as they navigate the challenging life of being a teenager blooming into adulthood. Register as a counselor at a local clinic to help people that suffer from mental health issues. You do not have to be a qualified counselor to give advice, perhaps, all those people need is a listening ear and a shoulder to cry on. You're uniquely qualified to do that.

This list is not exhaustive of all the various ways you can be a ray of sunshine to people who have not had an opportunity to be loved in this world. However, it can be a guide for you to start from. Expand on the list and invite your friends to join you, too, because if it is a group activity, you will have better accountability.

Different Love Languages

The best way to love someone is by loving them the way they would want to be loved, not the way you feel you can love them. We've all heard about the topic of the five different love languages originated by Gary Chapman in 1992. You will often hear people recite them off their fingertips without necessarily understanding why they believe that to be their love language. The essence of learning a person's love language is to know how to love them without letting your ego get in the way of your love. It is important to note that this is not a one-shoe-fits-all type of situation, and there is no need to choose a specific love language to the exclusion of the others.

Before you offer your love to someone, whether it is a family member or a work colleague, take the time to learn about what makes them happy. Be intentional about being that person to put a smile on their face. It doesn't matter how small the act is as long as it is from deep within your heart, and you do it selflessly. Here's a brief list of the different types of love languages that can help you love people better (Gordon, 2022):

1. Acts of affirmation

    Words can either build us or break us. We are always so quick to speak kindly to ourselves that we forget other people need it too. When was the last time you genuinely complimented a person for looking beautiful in their outfit? Positive statements such as that can help that person change the way they think about themselves and instantly make their day better.

2. Acts of service

    This includes doing things for people that they usually do for themselves but could use a helping hand with every once in a while. For instance, if you know that your next door neighbor works every day at 6 a.m. and they have to catch the bus to work, offer to drop them off at work every once in a while. Not only will it save them an hour from their commute, they will be glad they did not have to walk all the way to the bus stop. Acts of service are easier to do when you know the person whom they're directed at, but in a situation where you would love to help a random stranger, for instance, you know the homeless guy that always stands by the corner, try offering them a few paid nights at a hotel of their choice. Allowing them to enjoy the feeling of taking a fresh shower without feeling like an inconvenience to other people can change their perspective.

3. Giving gifts

This one is almost the easiest one of them all. There are, however, a few rules of gift-giving that need to be followed, such as, do not give in expectation of receiving from another person. A gift should be given with an intention of making the receiver happy and not merely feeding the ego of the giver. Always leave a note to let the person know how much they mean to you, how thankful you are for them, and how if they ever need help with anything they should contact you.

4. Quality time

Once again, every person needs the comfort of the physical presence of other people that care about them. Without any sort of distractions, we all desire to have deep, meaningful conversations with other people who can relate to how we feel. This also helps us to feel better about ourselves. When it comes to romantic relationships, an example of quality time is setting a time for sharing heartfelt feelings about how you can both love each other better. If your partner loves the outdoors, you can make this fun by taking a walk together while you talk about how your days were. Remember that the key to quality time is to make that person feel like the center of your world at that particular moment.

5. Physical touch

This type of love language is mainly specific to romantic relationships and family members. In a world that is so critical of non-consensual touch and respect for physical boundaries, caution needs to be taken. Besides the issue of consent, if your partner desires physical touch to be reassured of your love, always remember to hug her in the morning, or even kiss her when they're feeling low. This one should be easy when you're both in love.

Unlearning Toxic Love

Love sought, is good; but given unsought, is better. –William Shakespeare, Twelfth Night, Act 3: Scene 1, Line 153

Love has been defined so many times already in this book that it's almost as if it is a regurgitation to bring it up once again. But yes, the societal constructs of love have told the wrong narrative about what love should be. So, when people try to love others the biblical way, they are often met with rejection. There is also the issue of being raised in a home where love was not openly expressed, you have learned to hide how you truly feel about other people. This sort of stuff can cause emotional baggage which can hinder a person from maintaining meaningful relationships.

How do you know if the love you've been exposed to has been toxic to you? There is no straight answer to this question except that when you notice that you struggle to have long-term relationships. If you do, this should be the first sign that maybe you need to relearn how to love. Not all toxic love is blatantly toxic. For example, some people experience emotional abuse over a long period of time causing them to later struggle to understand when that love crosses the line to abuse. They do not realize it to be disrespect, for them it's just love. Such people need to notice the patterns in their relationships, some of the signs of emotional abuse include making excuses for the perpetrator and not feeling safe to speak up for yourself when you need to.

Some people who were sexually abused from a young age may struggle to maintain relationships. Due to the past trauma that planted a seed of mistrust, they also do this with everyone they meet. Unfortunately, this kind of trauma cannot heal on its own, if a person does not find psychological help, they will end up developing feelings of low self-worth—while also having a pattern of relationships that reflect their first sexual abuse as a way of numbing the initial trauma. There are a lot of online sources available to victims of sexual abuse, and if you know anyone that is a victim of sexual abuse, encourage them to report the crime to the nearest police station.

Finally, we all need to understand that the human brain has the capacity to unlearn unhealthy coping mechanisms, we should never limit our healing process to a certain amount of time. If a person has been sexually abused for ten years, what makes you think you can put a time limit to when this can be undone. Give yourself the grace to learn new, healthy ways to accept love and to give love whenever you're in a position to do so.

Practical Exercise

1. What was your earliest memory of what love should be or feel like?
2. Let's try a mindful exercise. Think about the person that has loved you the most. What aspects of yourself did you expect them not to love? How can you show this love to other people?
3. When was the last time you did a random act of service without telling anyone about it? What difference did it make for you not to talk about it? Did you feel more fulfilled or unappreciated?
4. How can you help spread the message of random acts of service to the people in your community?

Chapter 7:

Finding Purpose Through Love

In the movie, *Slumdog Millionaire*, a young teenage boy named Jamal Malik who had grown up in the slums of Mumbai decides to play the popular television game which is an Indian version of the American show, *Who Wants to Be a Millionaire* (2008). The biggest reason Jamal joins the competitors is so that he can impress a girl named Latika. Jamal picks lessons from his life experiences to answer all the questions correctly which surprises the producers of the show. They never expected a boy from the slums to know everything he knew. Jamal's love for Latika gives him purpose to push through all the hard questions, and when asked why he thought he won the game, he said because "It is written in the stars."

Because he trusted his gut feeling, he allowed Latika to be part of the game by asking her to answer the last question. Jamal's story is unique to him, fate decided that he would become a millionaire and all he had to do was follow his heart, the rest fell into place. While not all of us have the poor background that Jamal had, it is true that his character was molded to be resilient because of the tough circumstances he grew up in. He had a goal to win over Latika's heart, money just happened to be part of the fruits of his goal. Many of us have goals to merely make as much money as we can with no regard to how we can gain fulfillment from the careers that we choose to do. We forget that love should be at the core of whatever we choose to do in our lives. This is because when the driving force for a dream is mere selfish gratification, it will create an empty void after that initial high. It is only from following our true passions that we can share our God-given gifts with other people while making a living as well.

So, how does one know whether they are living in accordance with God's purpose for their lives? Society has conditioned us to believe that whoever is earning a lot of money is living authentic purposeful lives which are not true. There is a misconception that the people who are rich have achieved their purpose in life which can be misleading for younger people that are trying to find fulfillment from their work. Purpose is much deeper than the amount that reflects on your paycheck, it is the reason you were placed on earth, and it is that dose of dopamine you get when you are truly living according to your calling. This is why you find people that are extremely irritable at their jobs, they have no passion for the work they do because their goal is to merely get their bills paid. The unfulfillment from their jobs develops into self-hatred which eventually spills out into their relationships with other people.

Oprah Winfrey, one of the richest female entrepreneurs in America, with a net worth of $2.5 billion is currently ranked number 12 on the Forbes list of "America's Self-Made Women" (Forbes, 2022). She has spoken about the importance of having a purpose that is bigger than just making a lot of money. Oprah realized at a very young age that the salary she received at her first job would never equate to her value as an individual. After working several jobs that really drained her mentally, she finally found her niche at the age of 17, when she worked at a radio station and enjoyed it so much that she wouldn't have minded doing it for free (The Oprah Magazine, 2008). It was only after completely detaching her worth from money that she found true fulfillment in life.

Therefore, the first step in achieving purpose should always begin with having a goal much bigger than the temporary joy of receiving heavy compensation for a job well done. In whatever you set out to do, do it with such zest that if you were to not get paid, you'd still show up at work the next day. Only then is your purpose not to be paid, but to offer a service to the people. Finding your purpose has no specific timeline attached to it, some people discover their talents at such a young age that they build careers from them. While others take a lifetime of trial and error to finally find their purpose. And while it is sad to think about, some people die without having gotten the opportunity to find their purpose for being on Earth.

Know Your Tribe

The word tribe is usually used to describe a feeling of belonging to a close group of people who have similar interests, practice the same culture, and are very often related to each other. We were all introduced to various social groups by virtue of the families we grew up in. Every society has social distinctions that associate certain people with a particular group. For instance, there are 574 federally recognized Native American tribes in America, each with its unique culture and norms (USA.gov, 2022). Native American people are given names according to the tribe they belong to, they are also raised in accordance with their tribal practices in order to encourage them to take pride in their identity. It is from this initial sense of belonging that an individual forms their level of self worth. That person will then be comforted by the fact that they have shared experiences and, therefore, they can always have someone to count on when going through tough times.

Every one of us reaches a stage in our lives where we wish to create our own tribe, it is the reason we leave home to make homes for ourselves. The traditional sense of tribe has evolved over the years, a tribe is a support group with shared interests, for instance, joining a sports club in order to find an avenue to discuss your favorite sports without judgment or joining an addiction support group to ensure you remain sober. Seek out people that make you feel like you can conquer the world, people that remind you of the spark that you once held, and can assist you vibrate at a higher tone. It is not enough to merely know your purpose; you need to align yourself with people that are going to help you reach your goals and be in the right places at the right times.

In a society that has normalized the culture of individuality, it is getting harder to maintain these support groups as people are resorting to quicker methods of resolving their issues. While these online support groups might temporarily offer the help that the person needs, they cannot be used as a permanent solution. The first step would be to find a mentor who can guide you on how to find an active group of people that are working towards the same purpose as you. The next step is committing to starting the journey of discovering what your true purpose is.

Purposeful Careers

Pursuing purposeful careers and passions that are bound to leave an impact on the world. What qualifies as a purposeful career differs from one person to another since we all have unique talents and passions; we can never have a uniform purpose in life. We live in a society that is motivated by the culture of materialism, which they refer to as securing the bag. No one is talking about the importance of pursuing a career that aligns with their true purpose. May people fear that these purposeful careers would not be able to fully sustain them and their families. We need to look forward to creating a world where individuals are driven by their passion to make a change in the world and not merely make money.

Some people have a fear that if they discover their purpose early in life, they will have nothing to look forward to or work towards after attaining that money. What is a calling? In the Bible, we see a lot of the disciples were living a normal life before they were called to walk with Jesus, some of them were fishermen, the others were woodworkers. and others were just the basic family men. However, when Jesus called them, He required them to drop whatever they were doing and follow Him in order to be part of His ministry. Most of them did not even question Him, they just obeyed and let the will of God play out. They could have also worried about how their families were going to get fed, but they did not.

How do you know that you have chosen the right career? When choosing a career, take into consideration what you will be required to do during the course of your day; consider the flow of the day from when you arrive to when you leave. Does it reflect your personal values? The right career will not make you feel like you have to give up your personal values in order to fulfill your work roles. You should not dread sitting at your desk. In fact, you should be looking forward to doing the same thing the following day and for the rest of your life. If you are already working at a job and you're not sure whether it is the right fit for you, consider following your passion instead.

Another thing to consider is what your motivation is. If you're motivated to gain money from the job you do, what happens when this job stops paying you? And after you gain all the money you need, what will motivate you to remain at your job? However, things are different when you're being pulled into something bigger than you. You don't feel like you need to be rewarded for your work. This type of motivation will make you work better. You learn to review your definition of failure when you know that it's just another lesson. Transcend the need for approval, fulfillment is whether or not you feel intrinsically engaged in the work that you do.

When we learn to love selflessly, we realize the needs of other vulnerable groups of people in our society. There is no dream that can be achieved if it is motivated by selfish gain, love helps us find meaning in life. It is from loving others that we learn to live authentically and offer our gifts to the world.

Community-Based Social Impact Programs

Notice that the act of community service is viewed in the light of that forced punishment that the department of corrections usually gives to offenders. Some people think that volunteer work is the stuff we do for homeless people when we feel the need to or whenever our schedules allow. This is not a genuine way to give back to communities. Community work is more than just being altruistic, it is connecting your passion to someone else's need. For instance, if you work as a veterinarian during your nine-to-five job, take some time over the weekend to visit your local animal shelter and offer to examine the animals for free as a way of giving back to the community.

Pay attention to your outside world and take the appropriate action to make anything you see. You're driving down your home street and realize that the driver in front of you has thrown a plastic bag out of their window, your first instinct would be to be angry at them, but take a second to think about the fact that this person is that one percent of selfish people that do not value the work of the street cleaners. Instead of engaging with them in rage, park by the nearby street and pick up the litter yourself. The next time you see it happen, report the license plate number of the driver to your local police station.

Using Your Gifts and Talents to Benefit Others

We are all gifted in a certain way, and while some of us may not hold world trophies or be pinned on walls of fame, it doesn't take away from our God-given talents. A gift is anything that comes naturally to you, or with little to no training needed. There is a difference between a spiritual gift and a natural talent. That is a spiritual gift is received from God, while talent is usually inherited from one generation to another (Dy, 2020). The Bible says in 1 Corinthians 12:7-11 (ESV) that the Holy Spirit gives different gifts to every one according to its desires and belief in who deserves what gift, this means that we can never be given the same gifts because our capabilities differ according to our strengths and weaknesses.

To whom much is given, much will be expected, therefore, if you happen to be blessed with a gift of teaching, you cannot reluctantly sit on it and choose to do it whenever you please. These spiritual gifts can be taken away if they are not fully utilized. God desires that we use our gifts to draw people closer to His Kingdom. Think about the story of Jonah in the Bible–God called Jonah as a prophet and gave Him the gift of winning souls over to Him. But when God instructed Jonah to go preach to the Gentiles in Nineveh, Jonah refused to take up the assignment.

Many of us are like Jonah, we sometimes mistake our passions for gifts. Not everything that you enjoy doing is part of your God-given purpose for this world. The most important thing you will ever do for yourself is realizing which interests are self-serving and which ones can you use to bless other people. Although this may seem hard to do, we have been blessed with the gift of the Holy Spirit which is that still small voice that we hear in our most desperate times of need. The reality of life is we live busy lives, it is not easy to pick up on that still voice in the midst of the chaos. This is why each of us needs to make time for introspection. Explore your heart's desires and align them with God's plan for your life.

Practical Exercise

1. Describe a time when love motivated you to make a huge change in your life. How did the same love affect your dream later on?
2. Look beyond what you love, make a list of what makes you unique–the things that you most value. Sometimes the things we love may not be our purpose, evaluate that.
3. Where have you felt most fulfilled? What do you value? Realize times in your life you felt most presence, or the ability to communicate to others. Focus on the consequences instead of just the outcome.
4. Write about your dream career, what did you want to be when you were a child? How has it changed since you found out your purpose?
5. What gifts do you have and how can you share them with the world today?

Conclusion

Just like Jane had to go through a traumatic event to discover that she needed to unlearn the toxic religion that she was introduced to as a child, many of us wait for some huge life-changing moment to work on our spirituality. Jane had so many opportunities to heal from her childhood trauma, luckily for her, her husband, Peter, was an angel that helped her relearn what it means to truly love, and her daughter Nelly rebirthed the feeling of unconditional love in her life. The loss of her unborn child taught her that God can bless us and He can also ask for His blessings back if He believes it is not the right time for the blessings. Sometimes our human minds are unable to comprehend the workings of God. When we go through hard times, we blame God for things that went wrong. We become so impatient that we give the devil a chance to whisper shallow promises into our hearts.

God places different people in our lives for a reason. He knew that Jane would need a loving, loyal husband to guide her through her spiritual journey, as well as to also heal her from the trust issues she developed as a child. God does not bring suffering on His servants, but He is always around to help them get through the trying times. Nelly represents the new generation that has been set free from the bounds of selfish love by teaching her mom how to be more present in her world, how to be patient, and to have hope for the future. Jane has to be strong because her baby Nelly depends on her mother for survival. Because Jane's daughter reminded her of the good left in the world, she was able to relearn how to love herself in order to pour into her family when they were too weak to carry on.

The purpose of this book is to remind you that in order to love other people, you need to be able to give yourself the same kind of love. Therefore, speak to yourself with love the minute you wake up, affirm your presence "I am here, I am strong and I am kind," and never let your day take control of your emotions. Go back to visit the places where you faced the most trauma. It's time to learn how to heal from the past before it hinders you from having healthy relationships with people who actually care about you. You have to believe that there are good people in the world, and you have to be one of those good people. It's the ripple effect that will help to make the world a better place. Move in love, be slow to anger, and quick to forgive anyone. The book has defined love so many times that it is sad to watch any of the readers conform to the worldly standards of love.

As a believer, when you find yourself in a situation where you're not giving as much love God would desire from you, ask God to give you strength and the resources to be able to love His people the way He loves us. Be the living example of God on earth–when people meet you, let them be able to see the glory of God moving through you. God's description of love is very clear in the Bible, it is the purest form of intimacy we can ever afford other people. God knew that there would be times that we feel challenged and that is why He created us to be each other's keepers. The creation story says that God saw that Adam was lonely and made a woman for him so that he would have a companion. It is clear that the way the human mind is kind, we cannot survive in isolation. We need to study the word of God so that we can throw off our selfish desires, and only when we are fully clothed in God's gospel will we be able to reach out to other people in love.

This book calls for all of us to become spiritually evolved to the point that we cannot be shaken by small inconveniences. We need to learn to embrace the challenges of life because we were not promised a perfect life, God is busy molding our character so that we become better versions of ourselves. Our flesh makes us weak, which is why we are easily thrown off balance if we fail to keep a daily spiritual practice, however, God does not hold that against us. We should welcome all people that have wronged us the way God opens His arms to us when we sin. We should always keep in perfect communion with God, it is the only way we can keep floating amidst life's challenges.

We need to also learn that God is not limited to one religion. He is the same God that existed long ago. He has not changed, and we can all have a relationship with Him without feeling the pressure of being affiliated with a particular religion. For those that have found peace in their religions, keep an open mind about the idea that God is everywhere and He is God even when we are out of church. We need to stop seeking approval from man, and only seek God's acceptance because when we seek man's approval, we are giving preference to our ego which is self-seeking. It is also important to note that because Jane married a God-driven man and was given the opportunity to explore her religion without judgment. She was able to think of God in a broader perspective from what her father had limited her to when she was a child. Therefore, we need to be careful of the company that we keep because it can either draw us away from God or bring us closer to Him.

If you find yourself feeling a little challenged by the standard of love that has been set out in this book, speak to yourself with kind compassion. Know that it takes years of practice to get to that perfect measure of love–it is a journey, not a marathon. Give yourself daily challenges to help you monitor your progress and notice how you leave people feeling after you speak to them. Do you speak life into their lives? Or are you one of those pessimistic people? Love people even when they do not deserve to be loved because we are also sinners. Give up the sense of entitlement and learn to give back to your community. Do not expect the billionaires to be the ones giving back just because they have so much. God has blessed you with what you have, if you are too selfish to share it, He will take it back.

Meet yourself again from the evolved point-of-view by applying these lessons to your daily life. Ask yourself how your career is contributing to the society that you live in, find fulfillment from the work you do every day so that you will have enough love to give to each and every client that shows up at your workplace. You need to also realize that when you step out into the world, you represent God's love for His people. Remain faithful to God in everything that you do and spread the wonders of His love to the people that you meet. What may seem like a small answered prayer might be a miracle for someone that needs that hope. Jane thought she would never be able to have children and yet God used her loss to help her get to know God better, and through what seemed like a setback, her soul was redeemed. She discovered a whole new world after loss and was blessed with another child.

You might already have had a plan for your life, redefine that plan by asking God to show you His Will for your life. We can make so many plans but without God's approval, none of those plans will come to pass. Through prayer and fasting, you can ask God to reveal His Will to you so that you live in accordance with His purpose for your life. In a society that lives by their selfish desires, live a life of service to God's kingdom. Through your example, the generations that come after us will learn what the true definition of love is. Challenge yourself to perform simple acts of love to strangers who are not deserving of it, make it more fun by inviting other people to join you.

Finally, whatever you set out to do, do it with love without the expectation of recognition or reward from the world. Without love, everything we do is merely a manifestation of our ego and cannot bring any long-term good in the world. Amidst all the changing times, the loss, and the periods of harvest God is the only thing that will remain constant. The secret of life is learning to smile through the bad times as we wait for the sun to rise again.

References

Art of Living. (2020, August 6). *A Brief History of Yoga*. Art of Living (United States). https://www.artofliving.org/us-en/yoga/yoga-for-beginners/brief-history-yoga

Baronavski, C., Majumdar, S., Villa, V., & Webster, B. (2021, September 30). *Religious restrictions around the world*. Pew Research Center's Religion & Public Life Project. https://www.pewresearch.org/religion/interactives/religious-restrictions-around-the-world/

Bible Gateway. (n.d.). *Bible Gateway Psalm 19 :: NIV*. Web.mit.edu. Retrieved May 10, 2022, from http://web.mit.edu/jywang/www/cef/Bible/NIV/NIV_Bible/PS+19.html#:~:text=Psalm%2019%201&text=The%20heavens%20declare%20the%20glory

Bolinger, H. (2021, January 24). *Why Did God Allow for "an Eye for an Eye" in the Old Testament?* Biblestudytools.com.

https://www.biblestudytools.com/bible-study/topical-studies/why-did-god-allow-for-eye-for-an-eye-in-the-old-testament.html

Cherry, K. (2020, August 2). *Is Love Biological or Is It a Cultural Phenomenon?* Verywell Mind. https://www.verywellmind.com/what-is-love-2795343

Coffey, D. (2021, February 27). *Why does Christianity have so many denominations?* Livescience.com. https://www.livescience.com/christianity-denominations.html

Data Commons. (n.d.). *Earth - Place Explorer - Data Commons.* Datacommons.org. Retrieved May 10, 2022, from https://datacommons.org/place/Earth?utm_medium=explore&mprop=count&popt=Person&hl=en

Drumsta, R. (2020, December 7). *Does God Expect Us to Be Perfect?* Christianity.com. https://www.christianity.com/wiki/god/does-god-expect-us-to-be-perfect.html

Dy, G. (2020, May 21). *What Is the Difference Between Talent and Spiritual Gifts?* Christianity.com. https://www.christianity.com/wiki/christian-life/difference-between-talent-and-spiritual-gifts.html

Eckhart Tolle, & YouTube. (2019). How To Benefit The Collective Consciousness of Humanity. In *YouTube*. https://www.youtube.com/watch?v=KKW9GXsW-A4

Forbes. (2022, May 12). *Oprah Winfrey*. Forbes. https://www.forbes.com/profile/oprah-winfrey/?sh=5c4788b45745

Goodreads. (n.d.). *A quote from Eat, Pray, Love*. Www.goodreads.com. Retrieved May 11, 2022, from https://www.goodreads.com/quotes/116640-go-back-to-bed-said-the-omniscient-interior-voice-because

Gordon, S. (2022, January 23). *What Are the Five Love Languages?* Verywell Mind. https://www.verywellmind.com/can-the-five-love-languages help your-relationship-4783538#:~:text=If%20you%20find%20that%20this

Hart, P. (2019). *What Is the Mind-Body Connection? | Taking Charge of Your Health & Wellbeing*. Taking Charge of Your Health & Wellbeing. https://www.takingcharge.csh.umn.edu/what-is-the-mind-body-connection

Harvard Health Publishing. (2020, July 6). *Understanding the Stress Response*. Harvard Health; Harvard Health. https://www.health.harvard.edu/staying-healthy/understanding-the-stress-response

Harvard's Psychology Department. (2022). *William James*. Psychology.fas.harvard.edu. https://psychology.fas.harvard.edu/people/william-james#:~:text=His%20belief%20in%20the%20connection

Kentucky Counseling Center. (2021, April 9). *Ego Check: Don't Let Your Ego Problems Take Control of Your Life*. Kentucky Counseling Center. https://kentuckycounselingcenter.com/ego-check-dont-let-your-ego-problems-take-control/

Marder, J. (2022, January 28). Be Here Now: How to Exercise Mindfully. *The New York Times.* https://www.nytimes.com/2022/01/28/well/move/exercise-mindfulness.html

Merriam-Webster. (2019). *Definition of SOUL.* Merriam-Webster.com. https://www.merriam-webster.com/dictionary/soul

My Online Therapy. (2021, March 26). *What is your inner child (and why it's important you get to know them).* My Online Therapy. https://myonlinetherapy.com/what-is-your-inner-child-and-why-its-important-you-get-to-know-them/

National Center for Complementary and Integrative Health. (2019, May). *Yoga: What you need to know.* NCCIH. https://www.nccih.nih.gov/health/yoga-what-you-need-to-know

Nguyen, J. (2020, March 26). *7 Types Of Subtle Experiences That Can Develop Into Micro-Traumas.* Mindbodygreen.

https://www.mindbodygreen.com/articles/micro-trauma-experiences/

Oprah Winfrey Network. (n.d.-a). *An Exercise to Diminish the Ego | A New Earth | Oprah Winfrey Network - YouTube*. Www.youtube.com. Retrieved May 14, 2022, from https://www.youtube.com/watch?v=K19_yVtmJK4

Oprah Winfrey Network. (n.d.-b). *What Is Meditation and Why Should I Do It? | SuperSoul Sunday | Oprah Winfrey Network - YouTube*. Www.youtube.com. Retrieved May 10, 2022, from https://www.youtube.com/watch?v=NiRvFUlVOe0

The Oprah Magazine. (2008, March). What Oprah Knows About Money. *Oprah.com*. https://www.oprah.com/omagazine/what-oprah-knows-for-sure-about-money

The Yoga Institute. (2018, February 14). *Difference Between Yoga and Meditation*. The Yoga Institute. https://theyogainstitute.org/difference-between-yoga-and-meditation/

USA.Gov. (2022, January 7). *Indian Tribes and Resources for Native Americans | USAGov.* Www.usa.gov. https://www.usa.gov/tribes#:~:text=for%20Native%20Americans-

Made in the USA
Middletown, DE
01 January 2023